Robert H. Scott

THE FUTURE:

IT'S HERE! ?

NOW WHAT?

Beacon Hill Press of Kansas City
Kansas City, Missouri

This book about century 21
is dedicated to the wonderful family
who made my journey one of such special joy
in the 20th century and gives me delight as this
21st century begins:
Carolyn, my wife, best friend, and companion
for over 50 years (she must have been a child bride!)
And our children and grandchildren:
Vicki and Stephen, Heather and Holly,
Steve and Debbie, Robert and David.
It's family the way God dreamed for it to be!
In the tomorrow world that has arrived,
may you experience His specialty of
"family enrichment."
He is the grace-giving and sovereign God
for your life also!

CONTENTS

FOREWORD

by Jerry D. Porter

DR. SCOTT brings a wealth of wisdom to the assignment of envisioning a brave, vibrant church for the 21st century. He challenges us to be a multigenerational, interrelated, multicultural global church family. He is not willing that we diminish the significance of any Nazarene players but celebrates our unity in diversity. This book communicates powerfully with Christian leaders from each generation, helping us to prayerfully discern matters of *soul* that must not change as opposed to matters of *system* that can be adjusted to increase our effectiveness. With sanctified optimism he offers practical handles to help us *invent* the hope-filled future for this beloved international church community.

Dr. Robert Scott is loved as a visionary churchman, courageous missiologist, and loving husband, father, and grandfather with five decades of servant leadership as pastor, district superintendent, World Mission Division director, chairman of the Hiram F. Reynolds Institute, renowned church consultant, and seminar speaker.

This book is vital for church leaders who want to pilot relevant Kingdom-ministry congregations in the millennial community. This will be an excellent tool for church boards, Sunday School classes, and vision-casting groups. This material will also be valuable to leaders who want a missional revival among their constituents. His guidelines will assist any church endeavoring to bridge gaps that might separate us from each other, allowing us to face together the awesome challenges of communicating the Christ-message to a postmodern, secular world. Dr. Scott has done the church and the Kingdom a great service by bringing his wealth of knowledge, reading, and experience to bear on the opportunities and challenges we face as the Body of Christ.

At Last It's Here!

———■———

The best thing about the future is that
it comes only one day at a time.
—Abraham Lincoln

God is a safe place to hide,
ready to help when we need him.
We stand fearless at the cliff-edge of doom,
courageous in seastorm and earthquake,
Before the rush and roar of oceans,
the tremors that shift mountains. . . .
"Step out of the traffic! Take a long,
loving look at me, your High God."
—Ps. 46:1-3, 10, TM

This day's focus
on a dawning new century and millennium of time
gives sensitive and authentic spiritual adventurers
an amazing potential-filled opportunity
to experience discovery of the greatest—Him—
to become part of a new and better world
and leave a legacy of a better world in the future!

———■———

Dialogue in Real Time

Hello, A.D. 2001-plus. You're finally here!

Should I be nice and say "Welcome," or should I tell you what people are saying about you? You frightened us before you got here. One thing is sure—we're glad the wait is over. Just a little warning: you may not like it here. The earth is in quite a mess. One cynic says, "Not even God can fix this world."

Another voice announced, "He doesn't have to. We're smart enough to do it ourselves."

Still others believe that not only can things improve, but God will be at the middle of the project. And a lot of His friends will be helping Him. We all might be most surprised at what God does when He really goes to work.

As I think about it, I find surprising reasons to feel hope. Maybe, just maybe, God and His friends will do better than we can begin to imagine.

The Future Has Arrived

Preface

AT LAST the long countdown is over. We're now in a new century and millennium. We've met "the future" face-to-face.

What a relief to be past the late-'90s waiting frenzy! All the hype about a new millennium wore us out. At last, peace! A tombstone stands over the stillborn "Y2K bug." Few are grieving.

The future has brought dazzling luggage. Two of its buzzwords are _micro_ and _macro,_ the miniscule and the massive. The future will continue to focus on inner space (life sciences, genetic mapping) and outer space (exploring the universe). The two may even meet in surprising coalitions. We're designing space stations to be exotic hotels for adventurers. Others may be hospitals where human infirmities may be treated by weightless therapies.

This is a new education time. Terms like _time, work, recreation, home, family, money, vacation,_ and _life expectancy_ have new implications we must learn. In fact, most things will never be the same. Challenging? Thrilling? Scary? Or all of these?

The future has arrived and dares us to enter further. A recent book on new shapes of leadership opened with this intriguing line: "Don't read this book if you can't cope with risk!"[1]

Looking at the emerging horizon, we might be tempted to say: "Don't even keep breathing if you can't cope with risk, change, and other unknown surprises."

The future has arrived! Here are some of its heavy questions: How will change affect _my_ life? Can social disintegration be slowed down? Will life anchors such as value systems and inspiring character traits ever emerge more prominently? Is there a fulfilling spiritual discovery? Will yearnings for security and hope ever be realized? Where are we headed?

In this new millennium, we must scrutinize who God really is, what He wants to say to 21st-century people, and what He is permitted to do in the ongoing drama of human life. Such interest must be more than courteous confabs, but must be a seamless dialogue between thought and life, word and action, today and tomorrow.

Every culture of history has heard wide assortments of religious discussion. We still hear much, but it is often framed in narrow contexts of ambiguity. We hear religion is out and spirituality is in. Church is on the obsolete list, while customizing one's tastes for worship or the sacred is in. What does all this mean?

As changes gain momentum, what will happen to traditions of the Judeo-Christian God and His teachings? Humanistic philosophers admit the influence His words and followers have had in the past. But does God and what He stands for have a chance in the new world?

Before we panic and imagine that this century is carrying us into hopeless territory, we need a brief visit to the school of history.

History's curriculum is liberally documented with events, people, and years that show Almighty God's hand at work. To the objective mind, that curriculum gives convincing argument that we have a sovereign God, and that time's final chapter is already designed and indeed beautiful!

Here are some lessons to learn in history's school.

- *Lesson One:* Though God is holy and sovereign, having given free will to His human creations, He permits many things He does not desire.
- *Lesson Two:* However human freedom has discolored life, God gives His people special promises and love.
- *Lesson Three:* God is neither hurried nor delayed in fulfilling His eternal plan.
- *Lesson Four:* Despite evil's shocking powers, God can still ultimately make evil serve His purpose.
- *Lesson Five:* The powers and leaders of this world—good and bad—are all temporary.

○ *Lesson Six:* God's operational sphere, concern, and care stretch from the farthest point of the universe to the smallest organism within the universe.

History's most chaotic scenes reveal that God never gave up on His cause or His people. Egypt and Babylon were dark, but they were not the end. Calvary was dark, but it was not the end. The German holocaust and communist domination were dark, but they were not the end. A self-confident, affluent Western culture is in peril and imperiling, but whatever it brings next is not the exclusive domain of even its greatest technologies. Something else is involved here. *Someone* is involved here.

Michael Howard, Yale University history professor, said, "All we believe about the *present* depends on what we believe about the *past.*" We are wise to listen to the lessons of history.

The Bible confirms these. In the Old Testament Ps. 33:11 encourages, "The plans of the LORD stand firm forever, the purposes of his heart through all generations." The New Testament reassures, "Jesus Christ is the same yesterday and today and forever" (Heb. 13:8). The Psalmist summarized, "God's love is meteoric, his loyalty astronomic, his purpose titanic, his verdicts oceanic. Yet in his largeness nothing gets lost; not a man, not a mouse, slips through the cracks" (36:5-6, TM).

What a resource with which to walk into the unfolding days!

The future has arrived. A loving, faithful God was here through the chaos leading to this time. He will be with the challenges accompanying it. He will be nearby when today's future becomes tomorrow's yesterday. Everything changes—except God. His love and grace will never change. His power and sovereignty will never be inadequate for human emergencies.

We need a strong link between God's reality and the hopelessness of our world. God proposes, "Walk with Me as Abraham did. Talk with Me. When you have to cry, I'll cry with you. Let me give you a lifestyle that is a beautiful object lesson for an uncertain world. You will be *salt* to give this world new flavor. And you will be *yeast* to penetrate the world until your contagious authenticity makes others hungry. And you will be *lights* that shine in the world's darkness to help it find its way back home to Me!"

The future has arrived! Don't panic. Set up your home page on the Internet of life so every place you click on will yield deeper involvement with Him.

Before you move on into the "what it will be like and how to handle it" adventure of this book, read out loud, and contemplate these final thoughts:

God and I together can and will make it. We will form an unbeatable partnership through all that confronts me now, and through whatever lies beyond tomorrow's horizon!

PART 1

---■---

Is There a Road Map?

A new civilization is emerging in our lives.
This new civilization brings with it
new family styles, changed ways of working,
loving and living. Millions are attuning
their lives to the rhythms of tomorrow.
The dawn of this new civilization is the
single most explosive fact of our lifetime.
—Alvin Toffler, futurist

What, me worry about tomorrow?
I'm just trying to get through today!
—Ziggy

Consider what God has done. . . .
When times are good, be happy;
but when times are bad, consider [ponder].
—Eccles. 7:13, 14

---■---

Dialogue in Real Time

Hello, A.D. 2001-plus. Are you confused? Who wouldn't be?

What was right yesterday is wrong today. What was wrong yesterday is OK now. Has everybody's compass gone berserk?

Have you heard them describe you? You're called "the postmodern era." That's confusing, because what's "modern" isn't over yet. We seem to be in two time eras at the same time. Or is it three? What's happening?

Don't be surprised at the sights and sounds you find. They're puzzling. But don't panic. All of this confusion propels some interesting searches —for hope and meaning and values and God. Maybe God will use such times to prove He's still to be reckoned with. He has lots of friends ready to help Him. Many think this is exactly what will happen. And, you know—so do I!

1

It's Here, So What to Think About It?

IT'S HERE. But what's here? Who can define this new age into which our lives have moved? Who knows what to do or think about it?

Mixed within the beauty of new horizons are what appear to be ugly, threatening clouds. Will a severe storm strike?

In war-torn days near the mid-20th century, Winston Churchill spoke perceptive lines, framed in humor: "There are a terrible lot of lies going around the world, and the worst of it is that half of them are true." We smile and wince. How would Churchill describe today's conditions?

The human story has never been without its dark side. Today's threats of devastating computer viruses symbolize dark realities we've always faced in human settings. The "best of times" have always known the intrusiveness of "the worst of times." How to respond to this is one of history's burning issues.

Encryption was a buzzword in the late 1990s. It referred to scrambling certain data transmitted through the Internet so unwelcome eyes could not read it.

In many ways, the 21st century's complexity is like an encryption. Politicians and would-be politicians have field days with explanations and proposals. Religious prophets attempt to give insight. But conditions remain so complex that most cannot understand. It's as if social happenings have been coded in a new-century encryption beyond our grasp.

Such confusing environments offer inherent dangers and vulnerability. They have proven to be fertile ground for costly entrapments. When people are inclined to say, "Don't sweat it, ignore the scramble, leave it all with the experts (whoever they are)," disaster is near.

Of course we believe someone should do something. But we remove ourselves from the picture with such excuses as, "I'm not the best thinker on issues like this. I'm not a television analyst or a person of influence. I'm ordinary. What could I do?"

So excuse becomes an escape, and escape leads to ignorance, and ignorance becomes bliss, and the screen goes blank, and the computer crashes. When our expertise seems never to move beyond the realm of talk, watch out!

Realities at this juncture of history hold much irony. Information explosion has given us more data than any generation in history. Peter Large in *The Micro Revolution Revisited* states, "More new information has been produced in the last 30 years than in the previous 5,000. About 1,000 books are published internationally every day, and the total of all printed knowledge doubles every eight years."[1]

More than 800 new magazines began production in one late 1990s year. CD-ROMs with encyclopedic quantities of data rest at our fingertips. Massive data begs to be downloaded from our Internet servers.

But what happens to all of this valuable data? Does it leave us better informed or better functioning? Are we equipped to best address society's growing needs? We have the information and technical expertise. We do not have the needed *knowledge* and *action*—and *wisdom, es*pecially wisdom.

"CD-ROM technology is not a vacuous thing," Bob Dylan says. "But it's stuff that can happen without you having to participate. . . . It doesn't need any of my input. I wouldn't know how to use it if I had to."[2] We should ponder Dylan's statement in this day.

During the infamous Third Reich days in early 20th-century Germany, some of history's most inhumane cruelty was ordered by Adolf Hitler and carried out by Adolf Eichmann as they deliberately planned to exterminate the entire Jewish race.

On a cold 1941 morning, Minsk, Poland, was targeted for the brutal killing of 5,000 Jews. As Adolf Eichmann oversaw, the Jews were stripped and marched into a large pit that would become their grave. Gunfire began. Eichmann later wrote that most adults offered little resistance, as if they were reconciled with the idea of death.

The children, however, presented a different picture. They cried, clinging to their parents. In the blood-splattering chaos, he saw one woman hold her baby high, crying, "Shoot me, but take the baby!" For a moment, Eichmann, who had his own children, felt a flash of hesitation. Then the baby was shot, and Eichmann turned away.

Eichmann's diary reflected his conflict. "I scarcely spoke a word to the chauffeur on the trip back. I was thinking. I was reflecting about the meaning of life." Then he brushed off responsibility, "I was merely carrying out orders. No one thought things out in those days. After all, the people [destined for extermination] meant nothing to me. It was really none of my business. I was [only] a little cog in the machinery of the Reich."

Years after those tragic events, I visited Dachau, one of Hitler's concentration camps outside of Munich, Germany. More than 200,000 prisoners, mostly Jews, had been tortured there during World War II. The clay ovens still stood as somber reminders. No one knows how many people were killed An eerie heaviness filled me as I walked Dachau's grounds. I wept as I read inscriptions and reflected on the horrors that had happened in this place.

I wondered where the atrocity really began. When were the seeds sown that eventually sprouted into horrendous events? Could those carrying out the Hitler-Eichmann madness have imagined themselves in their role five years before it occurred? or three years? or one? What did they think as they implemented orders? Did any raise, or want to raise, protest? Or were the sensitized strands in their personality chords too jangled to have feeling left?

It's unthinkable we would ever degrade to the Eichmann level, but in our day, so notorious for its spectator lifestyle, we can easily live as detached onlookers. So much of the culture forces us into simulation skills. We watch the television screen. We sit for hours searching the Internet. We hear of poverty, homelessness, and hunger while we gorge ourselves with massive amounts of food. The virtual reality of our lives is neither virtual nor real. If discomfort badgers us too much, we can always change the channel or log on to another dot-com page.

In the rapid flow of such a lifestyle, citizens ignore their obligations to vote in elections. Church members stay away from the congregations they have joined. Church is kept the way it's always been, even though it may have lost touch with the world it is supposed to help. And people stay behind their own fences rather than engaging their neighbors with kindness.

It's here! A new century. What are we to think of it?

We're told that people now work more with their brains than their hands. Mass production is out, and innovation is in. Ideas, not machines, are valuable in the new century. Amazing opportunities. Surprising technological achievements. Striking diversities. Awesome demands. The world is now our neighborhood. The only constant is change.

New buzzwords reflect dramatic new realities. *Cyber age. Information superhighway. World Wide Web. Digital cash. Biosensors. Bionics.*

These terms have ominous wrappings: massive choices, depersonalization, confusing time pressures, growing insensitivity, a moral twilight zone. Where will it all lead? No one knows for sure.

This culture calls us to have good heads and strong hearts. We must frame our energies in self-discipline and discretionary choices. A time such as this calls for a strong Deliverer and a powerful yet merciful God.

This day has such!

Linked with God and with each other, we will do more than survive the times. We will beat them. And we will help our world discover the best answers for its cynicism and questions of "What?" and "So what?"

History's lessons are good to reflect on, for they confirm that we have hope.

The future. It's here. So now what?

2

Knock, Knock! Who's There?

THROUGH MUCH OF 1999, the world was bombarded with predictions of doom related to the Y2K bug. An authentic technology issue demanded remedy. But we also faced a frenzy that was not authentic. Legitimate businesses as well as religious extremists exploited the event. Gullible people became victims. It was classic misdirect, not without other historical precedents. The Y2K frenzy violated people's sense of well-being and honor. So will many other cultural realities on the 21st-century landscape. What these will look like remains to be seen.

To engage the most legitimate issues of the emerging century, therefore, we need a beginning point that acknowledges the dignity for the human family as Creator God intended it. It's a great time to return our attention to what should be most important: not technological issues, but people. Life should be about people.

Knock, knock! Who's there? People. People are at the door of the future!

The people issue gets complex. Talk about variety! Some of us have been around quite a while. Others are fresh to life. Some are tired from their journey, while others burst with anticipation. Some are frightened by realities of time and change, while others are challenged. Some are used to progress and modernity. Others are not. Some are driven by clear ideals and values. Others prefer no monitoring system. The impulse of the moment is their forte.

Factors within such broad varieties will determine what the face of the future looks like. Will it be renaissance or ruin? The answer will come out of people realities. This is one of history's profound yet simple lessons.

One of the best tools for understanding people is studying individual generations. Generations develop similar patterns of thought, value systems, and action. It's as if certain characteristics develop within the culture of generations.

Specific generations have become community coalitions reflecting their own common outlook, and their own influence and power. They also create and advocate specific agendas. Undoubtedly our media-focused and hyperanalyzed culture has helped cause this phenomenon. Read the newspaper. Check the television ads or programming. Go to a shopping mall. Get on the Internet. Attend church. In all these spheres, you'll find generations speaking their own languages.

When the different generations of my family gather, we notice these distinctives. A few delightful days with my wonderful grandchildren further remind me. It's not bad. It's just the way things are.

In many respects the variety gives delightful colors to life. But these colors are more vivid, more obvious, and more compelling than they have been at any other time in history. This can be an advantage or a disadvantage in the making of a new century and world. Which will it be?

William Strauss and Neil Howe have authored fascinating research, *Generations* and *The Fourth Turning*.[1] In these two books they examined 18 generations spanning four centuries of European and American history, to reveal a "history of the future." They believe such data carries predictable indicators of what may next emerge on society's stage.

Whether or not we support a cyclic nature in history and generation patterns, we see impressive evidence that each generation develops its own way of thinking and acting. Subsequently, each generation makes a unique contribution to the larger pool of culture, society, and history.

Social scientists observe that in each 100-year cycle of human history, four to five specific culture patterns surface. The 20th century saw five such generational groups.

Birth years for the century's first generation were from about 1900 to the middle or late 1920s. This first group is called the World War or GI generation, because so many of these people were engaged in the two world wars.

Many social scientists call the next generation, those born from the late 1920s to the mid-1940s, the swing or silent generation. This transitional generation was too young to serve in World War II, yet played a distinct role in transitional years of the Great Depression and World War II. These two diminishing generations increasingly receive a single classification today: the builder generation.

The third generation of the 20th century became famous as history's largest generation: 79 million persons. The baby boomers were born from the mid-1940s to the mid-1960s. The century's fourth generation group, following the boomers from the mid-1960s to the early 1980s was generation X or baby busters. This generation was only 60 million. The 20th century's fifth and final generation is called the millennial or net generation, born from the early 1980s to the beginning of the 21st-century years. Numbering approximately 80 million, this generation is also called a baby boom echo.

Each of these generations carries common characteristics of thought and life practice. Each made its own contribution to the culture and developments of the 20th century. Emerging centuries will likewise be shaped according to the thought and action patterns of their generations.

Already the 21st century reflects this, being distinctly molded by today's younger baby boomers, generation X, and the rising voices of the millennial generation. These are becoming culture architects of today's new world. Their imprint will be visible a hundred years from now. Will these generations carry this assignment as a sobering responsibility? Hopefully!

Nor is it for these alone, however. Input continues from every generation member alive at this moment in history. Cooperation and cross-generation efforts have never been more appropriate or urgent. Entering the future, new generational distinctives will continue to provide special designs.

For this sobering moment, a small cloud of hope is on the dawning horizons. Media and communication avenues remind us that world social conditions are degenerating. Television dramas portray generation X and millennial generation actors who model the rude, the crude, and the lewd. From such prolific dramas and the news accounts that bombard us, we might assume that the two newest generations are primarily interested in the grubby and the grizzly.

Wrong! In spite of image casting, we can find widespread movements that are in dramatic contrast to those flaunting indecency and rejecting value systems. Thousands of generation Xers are turning to God and becoming a core power in their churches and communities. Ten thousand Christian clubs meet regularly on high school campuses across America. Thousands of Christian teens annually gather at their school flagpoles to pray for God's intervention in their lives and culture. Such movements as Urbana, True Love Waits, and volunteer programs devoted to community improvements receive significant response from Xers and teens. As the 20th century ended, more than 13 million teenagers volunteered 2.4 billion hours in community work.

Furthermore, powerful shifts in the lives and thinking of younger generations will strongly impact tomorrow. While millions of young people lack basic moral perspectives that earlier generations took for granted, others show gutsy integrity that defies the dark tones of their world. George Gallup calls today's teens "the repair generation." Polls indicate one of their strongest wishes is that getting a divorce would be harder to do.

Strauss and Howe say, "This generation is going to rebel by being not worse behaved, but better. Their life mission will not be to tear down old institutions that don't work, but build up new ones that do."[2] Recent statistics support this speculation. Suicide and pregnancy rates among teens are down, and homicide and violent crime rates have dropped.[3]

In the last years of the 20th century, I enjoyed visiting more than 90 countries. I frequently stood in places where terrible national and political tensions and oppressions were exploding. I also saw walls of oppression collapse and entire systems disassociate themselves from decades, and even centuries, of dark philosophical ideology. I witnessed their efforts to emerge from the confusion and spiritual bankruptcy of political collapse, economic chaos, and human pain. *These movements were usually led by the youth.*

These days I travel throughout North America and less extensive areas of the world. In my travels, I see younger baby boomers, generation Xers, and the millennial generation modeling beautiful commitments to God. They confirm God's continuing hand at work in His world. They give me a strong hope for the future. My own four grandchildren are in that illustrious company: Heather, Holly, Robert, and David, along with their wonderful parents. How beautiful to see them embrace the mantle of responsibility to build a better future!

Revivals of past centuries have almost always begun with students on college campuses and in communities of those just beginning their life responsibilities. So may it be again. Hopefully, these young people will establish strong connections with God's church to best complete the task. Hopefully they will partner with Jesus. I believe this is their intention and commitment. They will become the new "mustard seeds."

In human history, Strauss and Howe note that a "civic generation" has regularly risen. These generations are driven to action, often by circumstances of the times. They change their world and leave a different legacy for the future. Thanks to their efforts, culture steadies itself, and for a while tired societies reap the benefit of their commitment. By Strauss and Howe's calculations, today's millennial generation is that "civic generation."

We are standing in what historian Daniel Boorstein calls a "verge moment," when we're on the threshold of a new world. Perhaps this dark and evil time will merge into a bright and revival moment. We can see enough signs to take courage and encourage those who are intentionally moving their world in a better direction.

The results will write a better tomorrow. These young generations are now writing this future.

Knock, knock! Who's there? The future. It's here. Now what? This as-yet-shapeless 21st century may be in for a wonderful surprise. So may it be!

> *Our Father in heaven,*
> *hallowed be your name,*
> *your kingdom come,*
> *your will be done*
> *on earth as it is in heaven.*
> —Matt. 6:9-10

3

The Label Says "Postmodernism." What's That?

MY SEATMATE on my flight from Kansas City to Atlanta noticed the religious title of my book and expressed curiosity. He introduced himself as "a criminal defense attorney, a secular humanist, a dues-paying member of the American Civil Liberties Union, and an agnostic Unitarian."

He had completed postgraduate studies and was obviously in a successful career. This man in his 40s exuded charm and self-confidence. I had not planned a two-hour conversation, but it became a stimulating engagement.

"I've known some weird Christians," he began. I told him I had also known a few weird ones, but that not all were like that. I suggested "weird" had come to my mind regarding some of the people and causes in his American Civil Liberties Union. He agreed and we laughed. Whatever distance lay between our philosophies of life and our life professions seemed to melt.

His next words were quite serious. "I've never believed a person can really know God. Do you believe they can? I think God is too big for anyone to know."

I conceded that God is too big for anyone to fully comprehend but added, "As concerned as He is about His creation, I believe He has found wonderful ways to let us know He is nearer than we imagine. I have discovered enough to erase my doubts about God's existence and to make me want to spend the rest of my life searching to know more about Him."

He asked, "What about Jesus? Wasn't He just an ordinary man, or a fable? How could someone possibly be part man and part God?"

His probing eyes revealed this as a point of special interest. I believe he was truly searching. "Yes," I said. "I believe Jesus was a very real and very special person born in the first-century world. In all ways, He was man like us. But He was also God, becoming man for a very unique reason and mission." I shared my conviction that He lived, taught, and was finally subjected to a horrible death. But that was not the end. He came out of His grave, proving He was greater than death and superior to the worst that could happen to a human. I added, "In my life I've accepted that He continues to live as a special and helpful Friend to me and to all who believe in Him."

"What are some of the things that reinforce this belief in your life?" he asked.

I told him how my life had moved from my being a frustrated, rebellious college student, trying to run away from the Christian influence of my family. But Some*one* pursued me. I found only confusion and discontentment in my own directions. When I acknowledged Jesus Christ and claimed Him as Lord of my life, I found peace and hope.

Beyond my experience, I reminded him that no figure in history had so influenced the centuries of time as Jesus Christ. I told him how I had seen evidences around the world that reinforced my faith.

In India, I told him, my convictions about Jesus reached special depths. India is the second most populous nation of the world, and it experiences the greatest concentrations of human suffering I have witnessed. These people historically follow the ancient religion of Hinduism. However, Hinduism has been unable to prevent the tragic realities of its people. My travel mate acknowledged that he had also seen that side of India.

I pointed out that thousands of Christians live across that country. Like their fellow countrymen, they know human suffering and face additional pressures from the influences of their country's official religious ideology. Often they are persecuted because they follow Jesus Christ. Yet these Christians of India display beautiful resilience and hope. They smile and sing and openly confess Jesus Christ in the face of national, cultural, and personal suffering. Without question, they know Jesus is alive and makes the difference in their lives. The darkness of their human environment only causes their faith to shine more convincingly.

"Nowhere in the world," I told my new friend, "have I seen people more convinced of Jesus' reality than in India. Such conviction can't be easily dismissed."

My flight mate listened with interest and contemplation. As the plane descended into Atlanta, he said, "I have one more question: do you believe in coincidences?"

"Why do you ask?" I inquired.

He told me he was not supposed to be on that flight, and that he usually traveled in first class instead of coach, where we were seated. "But I arrived at the airport early and was told this plane was about to leave. I took its one remaining seat so I could get to Atlanta a bit earlier. And I've had a two-hour conversation with someone whose philosophy of life looks totally different from mine, someone I would never have met except for an unplanned trip change. And I've liked the conversation. You were nice. You were not defensive when I teased you about Christians, and you were not pushy in your beliefs. You have given me helpful thoughts I will continue to examine. Can this be only a coincidence?"

"No," I said. "I don't believe it is a coincidence. I believe the big God you are curious about arranged this. I think He chose this to show you how much He cares about you and hopes you will keep searching for Him."

We parted, promising future contacts. I continue to pray that he will discover the dynamic Christ who arranged an intriguing two-hour flight for us both.

This young man's beliefs are typical of his generation. But not just his generation. It's the new label sewed into the life fabric of this new century: postmodernism.

While especially characterizing generation Xers, this attitude crosses generation lines. This mind-set questions, or has rejected, much that was once readily accepted in traditions of faith and humanity. Yet this mind-set admittedly searches, asking probing questions and acknowledging curiosity—especially about spiritual issues.

The conditions that birthed this mind-set were rooted in the life and culture spanning 200 years from the middle of the 18th century. Those years are known as the Era of Enlightenment or modernity.

Those years brought bursting achievements in economic and industrialized sectors of life. However, great gaps remained in the places where those achievements were practiced. The Western world was the greatest benefactor. Other parts of the world still held millions of people trapped in poverty and oppression.

With the opening of the 20th century, transportation moved from horses to spaceships. Communication moved from primitive means to cyber systems that give us instant access to people across the world. Jobs were metamorphosed as old systems and structures died and were replaced by new forms of occupation.

Many other prominent forces arose from the years of modernity, and in 20th-century culture, none was more repetitious or devastating than wars. The century saw 250 wars, taking more than 109 million human lives. In 1945, the United Nations was born. Ironically, as it was birthing to help nations live in greater harmony, simultaneously, nuclear power was being harnessed as a weapon of war. A total of $8 trillion was spent on nuclear power for war purposes.

In classic irony, during the first 50 years after the United Nation's birth, 150 wars killed more than 20 million people. How contradictory that such realities would dominate an age we were calling the age of enlightenment and modernity. How strange and inconsistent to have such overlapping realities!

My and my father's generation, both born before 1946, might have been displayed as modernity's finest. We worked hard to expand progress. We warmly embraced our traditions. Hard work was our gift back to life. We believed we could fix the ills of our world. Into one period of our lives came the jarring reality of the terrible 1930s eco-

nomic depression. It was preceded by the century's First
World War and followed by the second. Inconceivably, all
this occurred in less than a half century. It is a tribute to
these generations that Western world devastation was
not the end result. By sheer willpower and hard work,
and with the sacrifice of thousands of lives, those horrendous ordeals were overcome.

The enlightenment-modernity era belief system
pushed its scientific answers and priorities with pride. It
hawked survival as the reward of the fittest. People began to believe they needed material wealth to find happi-
ness. They were nurtured in the delusion that science
and human reason were life's primary components and
would eventually convert the earth into a grand utopia.

During this paradox-drama of reality, the younger generation became suspicious. The baby boomer generation
exuded disdain and cynicism. Anger gnawed at their con-
sciousness and conscience. They did not accept the belief
systems of their fathers. Seeing one 20th-century war
closely following another, carrying increasing powers of
human destruction, the hope that humans could ever
achieve peace and prosperity through their own means
suffered dramatic erosion. They felt we obviously knew
how to make weapons, but we didn't know how to make
peace. We knew how to improve fine structures for hous-
ing, but we could not turn those buildings into happy
homes. We could design compelling hierarchies of corporate and religious power, but those powers often func-
tioned without justice and respect. Is this what it meant
to be progressive and successful? If so, forget it. Baby
boomers (and others) believed we were failing at the
most vital points of life's meaning.

My Atlanta flight seatmate's generation saw the fallacy
before many of their parents did. He was a young baby
boomer. His generation and generation X developed different outlooks about what should be called progress. They
questioned their parents' materialistic value systems.
Maybe, they felt, this is all wrong, and it's time to say so.
Maybe a utopia for the human species doesn't exist.

Many baby boomers turned inward with their
lifestyles and refocused the 1960s on self-centered and

indulgent directions. "We won't keep fighting wars," they said. They burned their draft cards. A distant country called Vietnam would not taste their blood. A philosophy called them to tune in (to drugs or whatever else), turn on (to what your "thing" might be), and drop out (of a rat race that hasn't fixed itself in 200 years of "enlightenment"). Forget history. Reject authority. The institutions of society—government, church, home—deserve no more of our respect, they announced. Ideas about universal values and truths had proven ineffective.

So the seeds were sown for moral relativism in which each person makes his or her own rules or beliefs.

In the unfolding processes of this ideological revolution, social scientists saw the human race beginning a historic passage, leaving behind the 200-year enlightenment philosophy.

Something else was being born, but no one knew exactly what it was. Modernism was going out. We only knew postmodernism was arriving and humanity was making a historic paradigm shift. Futurist Alvin Toffler wrote, "We are living through one of those exclamation points in history when the entire structure of human knowledge is once again trembling with change as old [structures] fall. We are not just accumulating more facts. We are totally reorganizing the production and distribution of knowledge and the symbols used to communicate it. What does this mean?"[1]

In his book about cultural reality in the 21st century, Australian anthropologist Richard Slaughter wrote, "The industrial system which has reigned supreme on this planet for over two hundred years is coming apart at the seams. Something new is attempting to be born. . . . There is a spiritual vacuum at the heart of industrialized culture which makes it very difficult for people to resolve the perennial concerns of human existence."[2]

In their early years, many baby boomers insisted they knew what the problem was and could fix it themselves. They resorted to anger, and they loved argument. They were the best-educated generation in American history, serious, contemplative, and philosophical. "Prove it" became a favorite retort. They were logical. And as late as these early 21st-century days, the baby boomer generation still cannot rest, even in the new world they helped create. They do not trust much of the change they helped incite. A residual fear, if not suspicion, gnaws at their minds. They display this in fascinating varieties of expressions.

Generation X arrived, the children of baby boomers or younger members of the previous generation. True to the pattern of each generation developing its own distinctions, generation X has taken a very different route. Noting the flaws in their boomer parents' approach, generation Xers followed a less pugnacious road. They were in the first generation raised on computers. Witnessing massive shifts in technology and culture, they became sensory oriented, finding refuge in an entertainment culture with sound-bite thinking processes.

All this carried them toward a more practical, embodied life interest and logic, which is less combative and philosophical than the boomers. They did not embrace the boomer motto of "Prove it to me." Their motto was "*Show* it to me—give me something I can feel!"

Sadly, neither generational pattern in itself adequately resolves the dilemmas and emptiness of a postmodern culture. The search for answers continues in a world still holding strong remnants of both modernity and premodernism. The simultaneous presence of these very different philosophies poses little problem for postmodernism. Ambiguity is its hallmark. Relativism is its trademark. Truth depends on individual perspective, which teaches that we should not expect to discover only one validated center or answer. Many exist. So *centerlessness* is the ethos of postmodernism. And today's information explosion with all of its data is not expected to supply a savior. The postmodern mind is comfortable with T. S. Eliot's lament: "Where is the life we have lost in living? Where is the wisdom we have lost in knowledge? Where is the knowledge we have lost in information?"

The postmodern mind is ready to live with such condition. The more we learn, the less we understand. The more we learn, the less we really know. It's as though all the rules of the game have changed. What was true yesterday may not be true today. What was right yesterday may be wrong today. What was wrong yesterday may be right today. What was believed yesterday might not be believed today. Welcome to the world of postmodernism. No wonder it's a world where life moods swing regularly. Pessimism, if not cynicism, becomes a common characteristic of life.

Not all is bleak or hopeless, however. The very nature of postmodernism lives with a search underway. The postmodernist is looking, curious, and even hopeful.

My Atlanta flight seatmate modeled this. As a late-born baby boomer, he thought more like a generation Xer than a boomer. His uncertain, yet open outlook about God reflected this. So did his curiosity, his willingness to listen. After all, if truth is relative, another person's position is worth investigation. And, if the other person has "affable persona," perhaps that person knows something profitable, the postmodernist reasons.

Postmodernists, like my seatmate, may therefore make good listeners. And they may be viable candidates for interest in Jesus if they sense authentic faith. This postmodern day and doubt may bring previously unknown opportunities for authentic faith to be discovered—perhaps as no other century has seen.

Surely a redemptive, powerful God has this in mind! If only His own people will stay on the right course. In such a confusing world and culture, how will they do that?

How will we keep from drifting off course in a world besieged by quantum change? We need an unusually reliable compass to maintain accurate direction.

The future. It's here. Now what?

4

The North Star: Where Is It?

THE TRAVELERS now knew they were lost. The storm had lasted too long. For days they had not seen the sun or the stars. Thick clouds hovered, with rolling thunder and flashing lightning. The howling winds pelted them with sleet and rain.

With no compass to guide them and no stars as a back-up, the travelers could not know if they were still going in the right direction. Yet they had pressed on, urgently aware that worse winter conditions would follow this storm. A few days' delay could cost their lives.

But were they still going west? Who could know? They feared they were drifting off course, heading into empty wilderness where their dreams would never come true.

Then in a mystery beyond their understanding, the winds began to subside. In the pitch-black night smothering them, they thought they saw hints of clouds breaking. Tiny twinkling lights emerged. The clouds were indeed separating! Now revealed were the gorgeous heavens in their stellar array. The travelers knew what to look for. They found the Little Dipper stars clearly showing handle and cup. Their gaze followed a straight line from the formation. *They found the North Star.* They now knew which way west was, and east and south and north. This was their affirmation.

For centuries, travelers on land and sea have found their bearings in the North Star. This star has reinforced

33

courage, certified direction, and helped its followers avoid the catastrophe of being lost.

As travelers passing from the 20th to the 21st-century world, we need direction certification. Trying to negotiate the complex realities surrounding us, we face the peril of disorientation. This new future is unfolding in patterns of constant change, paradoxical contradictions, and out of a myriad of emerging trends. It is blurry with its ambiguous postmodernism label. Who knows what's best or safe or right? Many sincere persons fearfully wonder: "Am I drifting from the course that is historically validated by past experience?"

Collective associations of people such as in church traditions worry, "Are *we* drifting from the historically validated course?"

Is there some way to find confidence about our direction? Can we be sure we are not being misled or are not drifting into some damaging direction? Do we have a "kingdom of God North Star," which may certify our direction?

Such a question raises the issue of a "soul-statement" of truth for our lives: What are the unchangeables? Can we identify the bedrock that must always be maintained, and can we identify what is appropriately and allowably transient?

"Soul" and "truth" are concepts rooted deeply in both Judeo-Christian and Western world belief systems. They convey an intentional, specific frame of conviction. The conviction is that all of life comes from God and that He reveals His will and truth through time and human experience. This reality is beyond what is only mortal, temporal, or humanly contrived. It is found in the fabric of the universe and the geometry of life.

Soul is the trace and touch of God on human life, attesting that this human creation had a specific beginning, though it's essential being will never end. *Truth* is wisdom shared from the Creator's mind, enabling us to know how to successfully live. God intended that life-practice would honor our Creator here and ultimately bring us back to His eternal home.

Our most tangible source for enlightenment about *soul*

and truth resides in the Holy Bible. Its content has been repeatedly validated by history, and the best intelligence today can comfortably think of the Bible as "His story."

In the Bible, soul and truth are presented and defined. The Bible's conclusive summary about the soul is clear: every human life will continue forever, blessed in God's eternal presence, or cursed by a person's choice to live outside His presence.

And the Bible's conclusive summary about truth is clear: this book offers the wisdom and knowledge to guide one's immediate and ultimate journey, including help for decisions and disciplines.

The Bible, therefore, is bedrock. The Bible is North Star reality. The Bible is *truth expressed*.

Furthermore, the Bible reveals how *truth becomes energized*. Through God's Holy Spirit, the Word is brought into my being as I let it freely work in my heart and life. And God's work is a work of holiness, or wholeness, transforming spirit and soul and ultimately body.

The Bible illustrates and models *truth embodied*. Now I know how my life should play out on the streets where I live. My model is in Jesus' example among people of His day. Caring. Serving. Helping. Relating. Caring. Serving. Loving. Enjoying. Touching any and all with kindness. Always modeling integrity, honor, and holiness. Wholeness!

Further, the Bible admonishes *truth extended*. Life dies if I hug it to myself. To truly live, I must effectively engage in others' lives to help them discover soul and truth.

Finally, the Bible promises *truth effervescent*. Choosing to cooperate with God does not bring boredom nor reduce me to an automaton. Rather, it gives life a contagious sparkle.

Reflect how these become the five points of God's North Star.

1. Truth expressed—the Bible
2. Truth energized—the Holy Spirit way of living
3. Truth embodied—a Jesus lifestyle
4. Truth extended—reaching always to others
5. Truth effervescent—living passionately, contagiously

In the content of these truths, we will find the Kingdom North Star. If we look into the sky of our lives and discern such realities, we can safely believe we are on course. If a church can look into the sky of its endeavors and see such realities, it can believe it is going in the right direction.

The storm of secular and humanistic culture rages around us. It will continue to cloud the face of our world. So many confusions present false claims. Without God's Kingdom North Star to steer by, we might easily drift to marginal engagements that separate from Him, leaving us disoriented and ineffective.

God's authority and care can guide us through the cyber-age confusion. Better than the skeptical "So what?" mind-set of postmodern uncertainty is the "Now what?" mind-set that flows from a fulfilling sense of identity and anticipation of brighter days ahead. This discovery of God's ancient promise is available to the 21st-century world. "'I know the plans I have for you,' declares the LORD, 'plans to prosper you and not to harm you, plans to give you hope and a future'" (Jer. 29:11).

The future. It's here. So what? Now what?

PART 2

■

It's Here—So What?

Yesterday I was a dog.
Today I'm a dog.
Tomorrow I'll probably still be a dog.
Sigh! There's so little hope for advancement.

—Snoopy, in a "Peanuts" comic strip

"Meaningless! Meaningless!" says the Teacher.
"Utterly meaningless! Everything is meaningless."
. . . What a heavy burden God has laid on men! . . .
[But] I saw that wisdom is better than folly, just as
light is better than darkness.

—Eccles. 1:2, 13; 2:13

■

Dialogue in Real Time

Hello again, A.D. 2001-plus. You've discovered that we're in quite a stir here. We admit it. Our plight seems so complex that at times we're tempted to wonder if even God can fix things.

Life keeps changing too fast. A lot of the time we're not even sure what the issues are. About the time we think we have it figured out, someone changes the rules, and the game goes in another direction.

The world is moving so fast that while one voice says, "This can't be done," another voice already reports, "I just did it."

Can you help us get any handles on this kind of day?

A few really excited followers believe God will come through, and that we can grasp His hand through the speedy storm. Maybe it's true. We can't lose anything if we try that course. We may lose everything if we don't.

5

God Will Forever Be God

THE FUTURE IS HERE. Now what? Well, for one thing, God will forever be God!

While my wife and I were in Beijing, in 1992, a Christian physician gave us a six-foot parchment banner. A rich brown border surrounds carefully printed characters of a Mandarin Chinese text.

As I see this prominently displayed in our home, I remember the dining room of a Beijing hotel, where we enjoyed a delightful meal as this doctor and his family told us about their beloved homeland of China.

Dramatic and pain-filled changes had begun in 1949, beginning four decades of severe persecution and suppression for thousands of churches and Christians.

In the 1960s, Chairman Mao Tse-tung called his era a "cultural revolution." The bamboo curtain, preventing most of the world from seeing the pain and oppression, was imposed on China's people. Churches were forcibly closed. Christians were persecuted. Ministers and laypeople were often imprisoned for their testimonies. Bibles were burned. It was a terrible time in China's history.

In the late 1980s, political forces began to bring the bamboo curtain down. Christians outside China wondered what effect the years of persecution had on China's church. We'd traveled to China to learn the state of the church and what plans we might consider for helping the Church of the Nazarene further develop there in the future. The physician's family had been involved in the work of the Church of the Nazarene since its beginning days in China.

Their report was heartening. Thousands of Chinese believers had remained faithful. Now, we were told, Christians throughout the country confessed their expectation that God would bring revival to China, and they were offering to be part of that plan.

The parchment wall piece contained a personalized expression of the faith embraced by those Chinese Christians. The hand-inscribed Mandarin characters were the words of the Lord's Prayer. But within the text of the well-known prayer was a special addition of characters drawn in a different color. "What are these," we had asked, "and what do they say?"

We were told the aged father of our host family was responsible. He, too, was a physician. The 90-year-old man was the spiritual patriarch not only of his own family but of people in many villages where he had shared his medical and spiritual influence. He was convinced that Communism could not destroy God's work in China. He was committed to being part of God's kingdom through those dark years. He believed the country would see a brighter tomorrow. He was convinced God would remain God, even through all the discouraging days.

Accordingly, he established a custom with his family and other believers to affirm that expectation. When they were together, they always ended their fellowship by reciting the Lord's Prayer. But this patriarch instructed participants to insert a phrase as a special faith declaration after the petition, "Thy kingdom come." With emphasis they repeated, "May thy kingdom come!" and then, with celebration they would declare, "Thy kingdom *will* come!"

These added words appeared in a different color on our wall piece and reflected the stellar faith of God's trusting Chinese servants. *Thy kingdom come. May thy kingdom come! Thy kingdom will come!*

As new-century transitions are underway, we continue to see rewards of that faith and hope. During China's dark years, Christians remained so faithful that their numbers grew from 5 million to 50 million. Now, as many as 25,000 people daily are embracing Jesus as Savior. Though China remains under the control of communistic ideology, Jesus' kingdom is coming there, as significantly as in any other place on the earth.

In the final days of the 1990s, we heard legions of predictions—from the ridiculous to the sublime—about the world ahead. Cynical and humanistic people forecasted an end to evangelical Christianity. Some Christians worried that these views might be right and wondered if we had moved into a post-Christian era. In fact, one might wonder if these days are a new pre-Christian era.

Perhaps God has used the macabre closing years of the 20th century to launch a new wave of worldwide revival. We see evidence that more Kingdom advancement is happening than our self-sufficient 21st-century culture likes to admit. Not just in China, but all over the world, God's Spirit is moving powerfully.

In the 1990s, missions statistician David Barrett published a list of all known people groups in the world that remained unreached with the gospel—2,300 distinct groups. During the 20th century's last decade, world believers made an amazing thrust to reach those groups. As of January 2000, Christian workers around the world reported that each unreached people group had been embraced as a specific target group for evangelism for the first time in history. Considering Matthew 24, Bible scholars point out this may be the most significant biblical sign fulfillment to date affirming an imminent second coming of Christ.

Thousands of people in every country are experiencing God's power and love. As He changes their lives, they bear witness for Christ in other world areas. More than 70 percent of today's evangelical Christians live in the two-thirds world that once was largely unevangelized. Now this "two-thirds world" sends half of all the Christian missionaries who are being sent around the world.

Of every 1,000 persons in the world, 564 are Asian. An estimated 25 percent of the global mission force is Asian. Christianity is growing more rapidly in some parts of Asia —such as Korea and China—than anywhere else in the world.

Interestingly, churches from Asia, Latin America, and Africa now send missionaries to North America. Secular humanism and ethnic pluralism have turned this privileged nation into one of the world's toughest mission fields. More than 20,000 missionaries from the third world work in America. More will come. This dramatically reflects God's kingdom activity, speaking of His power and love all over the world.

Missiologist Dr. Ralph Winter points out that after Pentecost, the world held one Christian believer for every 250 people. Today we see one Christian for every 7 people. And, one of every 3 people in today's world identifies in some way with Jesus' name.

Yes, the needs are still great, and spiritual darkness still covers most of the earth. Everywhere, especially in once church-friendly North America, we find shocking examples of paganism, apathy, and darkness. America's media and political leadership have pushed this country far toward ultimate heathenism. Thousands leave North American churches every week, never to return. Hundreds of churches close their doors annually, never to reopen. Churches that once were vibrant are now stagnant —and comfortable in that stagnancy.

Dr. Henry Blackaby has pointed out, "The problem of America is not [so much] unbelievers; the problem of America is the [professing] people of God. There are just as many divorces and abortions in the churches as outside the churches. . . .Our gospel is being cancelled by the way we live."[1]

Blackaby does not leave it there, however. "The only thing that's kept America from going haywire worse than it has is the presence of [authentic] Christian community," he writes. "We're still salt and light . . . If things get darker in America, the problem is not with the darkness—the darkness is just acting according to its nature. The problem is with light. The light is no longer dispelling the darkness."[2]

But Henry Blackaby believes millions of Christian believers in America *can* dispel that darkness. Today's believers must respond to that challenge. God remains God even in such desperate hours, and He longs for His people to be the light for darkness, the salt for flavor, and the yeast for culture penetration.

Jesus forever affirmed this possibility when He declared He would always be building His church. In His earthly ministry He proved Divine power and love could work in the most hopeless circumstances. The ultimate proof of this was when He walked out of a closed tomb and proclaimed, "I am alive forevermore."

"The kingdom of heaven," He said, "is like a mustard seed." The Kingdom may seem overshadowed, but don't be fooled. He began with 12, His original "mustard seeds." If 12 authentic believers are in your group or community today, the Kingdom will come again.

God's people need to hear a great Bible promise: "If my people, who are called by my name, will humble themselves and pray and seek my face and turn from their wicked ways, then will I hear from heaven and will forgive their sin and will heal their land" (2 Chron. 7:14). The world's evil cannot prevent God's kingdom from coming.

God's divine vocabulary holds two magnificent words our troubled day should rediscover.

The first word is *sovereignty,* which means, "I AM GOD! I will never stop being God. My kingdom will continue to unfold as long as time lasts. No earth power, no earth person, no earth time frame can prevent that from happening."

Reuben Welch tells us in God's order of things, *sovereignty* means, "When nothing is happening, something is happening." God *is* working in this new century, whether or not His efforts are seen, whether understood or misunderstood. His work continues with or without "me" and even my church. Yes, He needs and wants us, but if we fail, He will still remain sovereign God at work.

The second magnificent word in God's vocabulary that a troubled 21st-century world needs to rediscover is *grace.* This great, yet gentle hope word affirms God's love for humanity's deepest brokenness and addiction. Even more, it affirms that He can and will do something about that brokenness. He can put broken lives together again.

In Mark 1:40-42, we find a beautiful story as Jesus encounters a leper, one of that day's excommunicated social outcasts. The leper confronts Jesus with daring words: "If you are willing, you can make me clean."

What an amazing statement of limited faith! The leper had faith in Jesus' *power.* "You *can* make me clean." His faith was uncertain, however, about Jesus' readiness to help. Would a person like him, a leper, experience Jesus' favor. "You *can* do this for me, but *will* you?" he basically said.

Jesus' answer was immediate and affirming and beautiful and bold. "Yes, you're right. I can make you clean. I have the power. But I have more. I also have the loving favor that includes even you and those like you, the most shame-filled and hopeless persons of society. Not only can I do this for you, but I will." And immediately the leper was cleansed.

This response from Jesus stands today. God's name for every millennium of time is "Grace-giving, sovereign God."

The future. It's here. So what? Now what? God will not stop being God. And God's love is ready to embrace and clean any life trapped in ugliness and hopelessness. God is not going out of business! He will forever be God. China is simply one of His many exhibits to prove this to the 21st-century world.

6

Change: Hate It or Love It?

THE FUTURE. It's here. So what? It's a day of inescapable *change.* Like it or not, we are forced into an ongoing dialogue with this thing we both hate and love—change.

Change is with us to stay, as the unavoidable reality for every dimension of life in a new century! Leonard Sweet observes, "It's crazy. Life has become one big blur. The velocity of change takes the breath away. Changes erase themselves before they even have a chance to take shape." And, he adds, "It's slower now than anytime in the future."[1]

In their book *Managing the New Organization,* Limerick and Cunningham wrote, "The idiom that says 'the only constant thing in the world today is change,' turned out to be the ultimate illusion. Even change changed!"[2]

The word *change* casts long shadows across today's landscapes. Looking backward we hardly recognize our own past. Looking forward we feel clueless about what to expect ahead. Is change a friend or an enemy? One thing is certain: Change is good for the aspirin and tranquilizer businesses.

We don't dislike *all* change. In some instances change brings us trauma. In other, it brings delight. When change results from our choice, and adds to our perceived life enjoyment, we love it!

Change was the dominant agenda item for the industrial revolution launched in the middle of the 18th century. Developments such as the cotton gin, the steam engine, and the railroads moved the human race into new directions. Over the following 200 years, modernity transformed the world.

I'm astonished when I reflect on how my life has changed. Early life for my family was on a 1930s Texas farm. We had no electricity or indoor plumbing. Telephones were rare. I was delighted when we moved to California and gave up kerosene lamps and outdoor plumbing.

As the 20th century began, transportation venues in the world moved from horse-drawn carriages to gasoline-powered vehicles to airplanes. As a young girl in the late 19th century, my mother rode in a covered wagon across Texas. She lived 103 years, and I never heard her wish she could return to riding in covered wagons.

Later, 20th-century changes continued to enhance life. We stopped opening garage doors by muscle and began using automatic door openers. Do you miss getting out in the rain, suffering back strain as you raise that door? And who would think of buying a television set today without a remote control? Further, most American homes have at least one telephone line. Many of us use extra lines for the Internet, fax machines, home employment, and our youngsters. We like to have these privileges.

In menu choices, in clothing styles, in home appliances, in automobile selections, in our stores, on amazon.com and ebay.com, ad infinitum, we cherish choices. We feel satisfied when we're in charge and have chosen the change.

Of course, not all enjoyed change deals with items or products of industrialization or modernity. Some interests in change concern feelings of power we have as we anticipate the direction of change. I have known people who pushed for a change in their church's leadership simply because they were on a power trip. That was pathetic.

So let's be honest about the subject of change. We don't hate *all* change. Some of it feels good. And change is easier at some ages than at others.

But many encounters with change shock us. Not all change is loved or easy. Just because it hurts doesn't necessarily mean it's bad. We need objectivity.

Changes in employment, in homes, in many family issues, and in church procedures are usually painful. But even though they deeply hurt, they may be best.

Carolyn and I have recently moved from our Overland Park, Kansas, home of 14 years to Placerville, California. We moved to be near our family and longtime friends. We feel this was the right thing to do, but we have had to reach into the deepest reserves of our being to survive the stress of this change.

I've even compiled a new list of "Life Mottoes to Aid the Retention of Sanity When You Move Across Country at Age 70," which I keep accessible at all times. Here are a few of my profound philosophic mottoes to get me through the stress of a major change:

- Next time I'll do this when I'm 25 years old.
- Next time I'll have the Robot Moving Company do this while I go to Bangkok.
- So help me, there will never be a next time.
- Yes, you can survive chaos.
- This can wait another day.
- It's bad, but not fatal.
- There's always tomorrow.
- Three months (or is it 12) and then comes the final unpacked box.
- I've changed my mind—not about moving, but about what I should be keeping in life.
- This, too, shall pass.
- Be still, my soul.

I've even learned to talk to boxes and cluttered rooms. I say things like "Wait your turn or I'll put you out with the trash." "I thought I got rid of you 20 years ago." "Yes, keep holding that, I will need it in the year 2100."

During this time of confusion, I've learned the importance of keeping a sense of humor. And how important it is to maintain a nutritious diet. And to get enough sleep. And to stay connected with people around me. And to commune with God! And, once in awhile, to go ahead and cry, and say, "Father, please help me, otherwise I'll crash and burn."

Change is not easy. But we can find ways to survive, even as change keeps changing!

Churches meet change with various responses. Not all changes in the church are bad. Some are welcomed. Every maturing friend of church knows that. Ironically, in church settings some of the most emotional crusades are conducted against change. If we resist change in church, while we practice change in other areas of life, we're being contradictory, and this may reflect on our maturity or integrity.

One young pastor told me, "You talk about getting the church into the 21st century. My church is still in the 1940s." His expression revealed the pain he carried from his congregation's unwillingness to be realistic.

Such congregations must distinguish between the "soul" of the church and the "systems" of the church. Church soul is the nonnegotiable, biblical, and doctrinal truth we embrace. Church systems, not soul, can and must change. These are procedures such as organizational structures, programs, methods, schedule, and service design. Times change, and our systems need constant reconfiguration to effectively reach people. If we approach an exploding tomorrow with only the systems and procedures of yesterday, we invite failure and premature death.

Shifting the way we do things is not only permissible but prudent. We should insist on programs, schedules, organizational structures, and music variety that serves our purpose. Changing the times or days of church services; varying the program order to increase interest; reducing the number of committee and board meetings to give more time to mission—all such sensible change can increase a congregation's effectiveness. We should not automatically resist new systems or meet them with a "jump on the bandwagon without thinking" attitude. They should be carefully, fairly and prayerfully considered, and then engineered for results.

At few points are churches experiencing more conflict today than around music type and worship expression. Some congregations clearly assert that they offer a "traditional" worship service or a "contemporary" worship service. Nothing is necessarily wrong with that. It implies their target group they have chosen or means they think they are in a community where the dominant resident taste justifies their action. Some congregations have reached thousands of worshipers with such emphasis.

Such specificity, however, is not necessarily best, or possible, for every congregation. Most congregations have a variety of attenders and must structure the church more diversely. Others may lack the resolve or resources for such exclusive ministry. This issue may cause heartfelt debate within a church.

The solution may be less elusive than we realize. The 21st-century culture of constant change is increasingly skeptical of an either-or menu and is more likely drawn to a both-and menu. With cultural feet firmly planted in relativism, postmodernists do not value arbitrariness. Accordingly, many effective churches resolve music and worship issues with an inclusive style that is balanced and blended, not exclusive.

The purpose of music and worship is to connect a person with God. That comes from prayer and openness, not because the service is contemporary or traditional. Contemporary or traditional are matters of taste and training. We sell our grace-giving, sovereign God short if we presume He can only reach sincere worshipers through one method.

In a sensible society people do not force their tastes on others. God has called us to relate lovingly to each other. I ask you to respect my worship style. I must do the same for you. And we can learn from each other. We can use multiple expressions to include everyone possible in our quest for connection with God. This broadens our own tastes and our understanding of others.

In Maine, I met a radiant new Christian. She was an Xer in her late 20s. She told me how her life was enriched by her relationship with God and with others in the church. She had come to that church from a pagan lifestyle. She knew nothing about worship. At first the hymns seemed dull. The music she knew was loud and filled with percussion. She liked the church music better when it matched her taste.

But in this congregation, a hymn and quiet song of preparation for prayer always followed moving choruses.

Over time, she began to notice the words in the hymns. She felt near to God as the quieter songs prepared her to enter His presence. She said, "My church has broadened my music tastes and my desire for authentic worship."

I realized I have experienced a similar broadening of music tastes listening to her. Through the contemporary praise music brought into the church, I have learned new expressions of worship. The joyful, biblical choruses sung so enthusiastically by younger worshipers have grasped me. I am energized as I observe their radiant faces, see their hands lifted in bold witness, and even watch their bodies move with the beat of spiritual enthusiasm.

Blended music and worship style has spiritually enriched and educated both my new generation X friend and me. Isn't that what God has in mind? Isn't that what He hoped would happen from the unsettling change that has forced new dialogue and prayer into His congregations? I believe it is! And I will cooperate that it may continue.

In the most effective churches I visit, this inclusiveness of worship and music is vital to health and growth. If people seek understanding and let openness prevail, and if they allow our grace-giving, sovereign God to reign, something will happen.

Of course the principle applies in other areas.

On the main street of the future, we face heavy questions. Will we practice objectivity as we see change? We have learned to live with change in vocation, in our addresses, educational expansions, life improvements, entertainment, and other areas. Surely change in the church is not an impossible exception. Surely in the crucial issues of understanding and accommodating generation differences, of impacting this postmodern world with the gospel, we can make change work for us—not against us. The systems must change—not the soul. And the systems will change, or our churches will die!

The marvelous old hymn "Be Still, My Soul" proclaims, "In every change, He faithful will remain." Our grace-giving, sovereign God will help us through these transitional confusions.

The future. It's here. So what? Now what?

7

Trends: Road Markers That Reveal Tomorrow

I CAN BUY a potato that's already baked, a salad that's already mixed, a steak that's already cooked, and a dessert that's already prepared. All at my nearby grocery store. Yes, my grocery store still sells those items uncooked and unprepared.

More than a decade ago grocery stores moved from merely supplying ingredients of meals to also assembling those ingredients. People who study social movements saw an emerging change that would impact the food industry. Fast-food menu limitations were getting boring. Consumers wanted wider choices of prepared food to take home and eat. Nor did the trend suggest the fast-food industry would go out of business: 7 percent of all Americans will eat at the golden arches today!

Studying food consumption, however, analysts noted that by 2020 57 percent of all food dollars in America would be spent on prepared food.

Entrepreneurs saw potential for a new food supply industry that would create a nutritionally balanced meal offered at places like my grocery store's delicatessen. Welcome to "Home Economics 101" in the 21st-century world. Getting in early on a trend like this is one way to become a millionaire.

In this future that has arrived, we can identify many trends encompassing every aspect of thought and life. Trends are more than "fad tornadoes" here today and gone tomorrow. They are movements that shape culture and become road markers to reveal what tomorrow will look like.

Shakespeare said, "What's past is prologue." Trends, as they rise out of yesterday's ideas and today's interests, are indeed a prologue of tomorrow. Gerald Celente of Trends Research Institute says, "Tracking trends is a way of seeing where we are, how we got there, and where we're going."[1]

Living in the sketchy "So what?" world, we should watch trends. Some are encouraging, deserving our cooperation and support. Others menace our prized values. Trends usually begin in small coalitions of a cultural interest or sociological practice. They may gather rapid momentum and predict their own future.

Here are a few of the trends we need to examine.

- *The trend to redefine life.* In Judeo-Christian tradition, life is sacred. But abortion and euthanasia are not-so-subtle redefining techniques. The World Health Organization estimates 45 million babies are aborted annually. Euthanasia is increasingly favored in certain countries.

- *The trend to redefine acceptable entertainment.* This day has popularized the rude, the crude, and the lewd. By the time children are 18 years old, they may have seen 200,000 violent acts on television, including 26,000 murders and 40,000 rapes. In one recent year, only 2.9 percent of the movies produced received a G rating. Sixty-six percent were rated R. Real-life dramas, like *Survivor* and its planned sequels, replace simulated dramas. What effect will this trend have on human sensitivities?

- *The trend toward media sovereignty.* Today's media has long since left the role of reporting and is engaged in an unapologetic crusade to conform human thinking to the whims of humanistic philosophy. One study reveals that 87 percent of media leaders have nothing to do with church. Where will this trend take us?

- *The trend of judiciary to rewrite laws rather than in-*

terpret law. A plethora of hostile rulings against Christian beliefs have been handed from local to supreme court levels. To rewrite rather than interpret law is dramatically beyond our founding fathers' intent in our country.

○ *The trend to redefine the nature of human work and vocation.* World culture is moving from industrial and hierarchical society to entrepreneurial and informational society. How will this impact home, family, and church? The 24-7-365 lifestyle is part of this trend. Commerce continues around the clock, and around the world. Less than one-third of working Americans hold traditional Monday through Friday employment. How will this ultimately affect family, society, and church?

○ *The trend of a shrinking middle class and a widening gap between the rich and the poor.* Massive corporations are reducing their workforces while their CEOs take millions of dollars in pay increases. In the late 1990s, corporate CEO pay increases exceeded 18 percent while white-collar workers averaged 4.2 percent and factory employees averaged 1 percent. *U.S. News and World Report* states that 1 percent of the United States population holds 40 percent of the nation's household wealth. *Fortune Magazine* acknowledged that the United States population is increasingly segregated by income level. How might such a trend eventually recolor life?

○ *The trend of a rising median age in the world.* In 1900 the world median age was 20. By the end of the century, it was 25. By the middle of this new century the median age will be 42. Demographers speak of a population implosion. America is dramatically affected by a middle-aging trend in which median age is near 40. Life expectancy has increased for the builder generation. The huge baby boomer generation is approaching retirement. It's hard to overstate the effects of this trend on economics, community lifestyles, and church programming.

○ *The trend to redefine "family."* In the 1990s nontraditional households grew more rapidly in North America than traditional households. In 1970, 15 percent of children lived with a single parent, compared to more than 25 percent today. Only 47 percent of Americans now say it is wrong for a child to be born out of wedlock. Half of the couples marrying today have lived together (although they also have a 33 percent higher prospect for divorce).

One quarter of all households in North America are now single households. Where will this trend eventually lead?

○ *The trend to broaden the definition of acceptable sexual behavior.* Sexual intimacy outside of marriage is now normal throughout the world. Children learn about birth control in schools, with little moral reference. Television and movies dramatize aberrant sexual practices, and biblical sacredness is forgotten. At legislative levels of government, homosexual lobbyists are powerful and rich. They incessantly pressure legislators to legitimize same-sex marriage and adoption. This trend to redefine traditional family and marriage threatens the very stability of Western society.

○ *The trend to pluralize the Christian faith.* Two million Muslims and a million each of Hindus and Buddhists are now part of America. The historic dominance of Judeo-Christian belief systems is changing. This trend has more momentum because the postmodern mind believes all religions hold some potential good and are worth drawing from. How believers respond to this trend is crucial for our religious climate. The Christian response must not be closed or arrogant. Jesus' followers need to face their pluralistic culture with the conviction of Acts 4:12: "Salvation is found in no one else, for there is no other name under heaven given to men by which we must be saved."

We can acknowledge that other religions have sincere worshipers. We must model Jesus, remembering that people will only be won to Christ through patience, kindness, and authentic examples. We will not win them with skillful words or a belittling tone. There's a saying: "Don't tell someone their stick is crooked. Just lay a straight one alongside theirs." We face the urgency of responding to this pluralism with Christlikeness.

Christians should meet many trends with active countermeasures. Other trends, however, are surprising sources of encouragement and call for affirmation.

One of today's most astute social analysts is Faith Popcorn. Her organization, BrainReserve, serves as marketing consultants for many Fortune 500 companies. Faith Popcorn calls the study of trends a "Brailling" of culture to discern the shapes of the future.

In her book *Clicking* she highlights a strong trend in today's culture: *"The quest for an anchor."* There is so much confusion and bad news, Popcorn acknowledges, reflecting a society that is "adrift." She has discovered, however, that people are digging for something to give them an "anchor and a hope." She identifies current interests in antiques and genealogies as evidences of this trend. A woman of Orthodox Jewish faith, Popcorn believes a "relationship with the Divine" is the ultimate means by which people will find the anchor they seek. She identifies a search for righteousness and for roots as evidence that Americans are ripe for a "spiritual revival."[2]

The future. It's here. So what?

The emerging trends around us are road markers revealing what tomorrow may be. May we remain alert to challenging trends that would take us to more pain-filled tomorrows and align instead with those that add hope and stability to the future. It is the intent of our grace-giving sovereign God that we engage our culture as salt and yeast and light.

8

Paradox: Things Aren't Always What They Seem

A CUTE FABLE has floated on the Internet.

A senior angel is taking a junior angel on an earth-orientation trip to show how angels work. Traveling incognito they spend the night in a wealthy family's home. The family refuses to let them stay in the guest room, but sends them to sleep in the cold basement. As they prepare their beds on the hard floor, the senior angel repairs a hole in the wall. When the junior angel asks "Why?" the senior angel mysteriously replies, "Things aren't always what they seem."

The next night the angels visit the house of a poor, hospitable farmer and his wife. The old couple shares their scarce food and gives their own bed to the guests. When the sun rises the next morning, the angels find the farmer and his wife in tears. Their only cow lies dead. Milk from this cow was the couple's only source of income.

The angels extend sympathy and then leave. Now the junior angel angrily asks the senior angel. "Why did this happen? The rich man had everything, and you helped him by repairing his wall. The poor couple shared all they had with us, and you let their cow die."

Then the senior angel explains. "In the basement of the mansion, I noticed a rich vein of gold behind the hole in the wall. Since the owner would not share his good fortune, I sealed the wall. He will never find it. Last night as we slept in the farmer's bed, the angel of death came for the farmer's wife. I told the angel to take the cow instead. You see, things aren't always what they seem."

The 21st-century world confronts us with a contradicting, confusing plethora of sights and sounds. As in the angel story the haves seem to gain more. The have-nots lose the little they possess. Has justice disappeared? Are things what they seem? A search for understanding continues. Could a powerful Providence be at work even in chaotic hours?

In *The Age of Paradox,* Charles Handy writes about the contradictions we encounter as we try to make sense of life around us. Handy notes that so many good intentions seem to have unintended consequences and so many formulas for success carry "stings in their tail." He writes, "Sometimes it seems that the more we know, the more confused we get; the more we increase our technical capacity, the more powerless we become. With all our sophisticated armaments we can only watch impotently while parts of the world kill each other. We grow more food than we need but cannot feed the starving. We can unravel the mysteries of the galaxies but not of our own families."[1]

What is really happening in such a unique time of history when life experiences carry us through so many puzzling adventures?

Think about it. Around us today a new world is being born.

- It is a world with amazing technological developments.
- It is a world with vast information expansion.
- It is a world with fewer political and geographical borders.
- It is a world with constant cultural changes.
- It is a world of unending paradigm shifts. So much is so bright, yet so much remains so dark.
- Amazing technological developments have not brought peace.
- The vast information explosion has not given us wisdom.
- Fewer geographic and political borders bring us more strife and war.
- Constant cultural changes elevate life quality for some and denigrate life quality for others.
- And the rules seem always to be changing.

As one of the most privileged nations in the world, America seems to witness an ever-growing enmity toward its earlier Judeo-Christian beliefs. Some "pagan" world nations appear more open to Jesus' teachings than America is. William Bennett observes, "A group of students can by law get together and advance a Marxist revolution, discuss different kinds of drugs to take, talk any kind of deviant lifestyle, but what they cannot do is say 'our Father which art in heaven.'"

Social and political leaders with humanist agendas push to reduce Christian influence. Hostile judicial rulings are enforced beyond anything that our nation's founding fathers could have imagined. Political leaders who defend moral principles are stereotyped as "religious right-wing extremists" and are forced out of office. Roy Moore, circuit judge for the 16th Judicial District in Alabama, notes, "Politicians can do just about anything in public but pray . . . They can survive scandal and immoral conduct, but they suffer ostracism and worse once they are labeled members of the 'Religious Right.'"[2]

Yet amid these public prejudices, we find an amazing paradox. Americans, with people in many other nations, show more interest than ever in the subject of God, Jesus, heaven, hell, prayer, and spiritual things.

Gallup polls reveal that in 1994, 58 percent of Americans wanted to grow spiritually. As 2000 came, that figure rose to 82 percent! *Newsweek*'s May 8, 2000, issue reported that 78 percent of American teenagers say religion is important to them, though only half attend church services regularly. "There is a hunger," the article said, "for guidelines that parents haven't offered." It is a fascinating paradox that the same Americans who ignore church show a fascination with Jesus.

For two years in a row, 1999 and 2000, *Newsweek* gave a March issue cover to Jesus and carried extensive articles on His influence in the world. In May 2000, a weeklong miniseries on Jesus received peak viewing on CBS.

We can find documentation that all over the world, God's Spirit is moving with power and fruitfulness. A secular media seldom reports such but even in pagan America more is happening than we realize as God works through traditional and nontraditional avenues. A spiritual stirring is occurring in many denominations. Powerful movements are flowing across denominational lines.

As I travel, I constantly meet men and women who have recently emerged from lives of paganism. They are making sincere commitments to the God who has set them free. Interestingly, many of them cannot identify all the elements that brought their spiritual discovery. It reflects how our grace-giving, sovereign God reaches through unsuspecting avenues to reveal himself.

In Connecticut, a 38-year-old man named Bill said, "I was an alcoholic, a drug-using truck driver who had done it all! One December morning, I knew I needed to change. That afternoon I apologized to a friend for having hurt him. He asked why I was doing this. I said I was not sure. I felt God was beginning to change my life, yet I knew nothing about God." Shortly after this, Bill came to an awareness of sins forgiven.

We can see so much rampant evil in the world, but let us not be blinded to the fact that God remains at work.

Charles Handy observes that we need to do more, however, than just recognize the paradox conditions that exist. By taking a stand on the brighter side, we can help move our world into directions of improvement.

Authentic Christians manage the paradox times toward improvement as they model the ever-flowing hope in Jesus Christ. Authentic believers manage the paradox times as they believe God will always be God, even in an evil world. They manage the paradox times and are seen not just as those who point out problems, but as carriers of solutions. They manage paradox times as they become salt-light-yeast impacting their hostile world. They direct paradox times toward becoming better by using spiritual gifts and grace.

Authentic Christians manage the paradox times as they claim the angel's words in their own disasters. With God as guide, they believe "Things are not always what they seem!" Our sovereign God is still at work in all of this world's "so whats?" and He will not rest until His kingdom comes and His will is done on earth and in heaven.

The future. It's here. So what? Things are not always what they seem. *Grace-giving-sovereign-God is at work!*

9

Anytime Is a Good Time for New Beginnings

THE FUTURE. It's here. Now what?

A retired salesman stood in our church to give articulate testimony of his conversion to Jesus Christ. His wife's recent sickness and death made him acknowledge a need for something beyond his abilities. Jesus became real, forgave his sins, and transformed his life. With sparkle he affirmed his faith, standing as a witness that new life can begin even at 75 years. He made a beautiful discovery: Anytime is a good time for new beginnings with God.

The 21st century sensitizes us to beginnings. We do not start new centuries often, and new millennia are all but impossible to think about! Beyond the uniqueness of seeing a new century and millennium begin, however, may we discover that anytime is a good time for new beginnings with God—whatever the quagmire of human despair, whatever the overwhelming demands of life.

My parents believed that. Their faith started early in their lives. As their futures unfolded, however, they proved how people of strong faith can make new starts in other areas, such as vocation or geography.

To better their family's future after the 1930s depression-driven poverty, my parents loaded scant earthly possessions in a tired old Pontiac with dangerously worn tires and patched inner tubes. They followed a narrow highway from the dust bowl of Texas to California. We could have helped John Steinbeck write *The Grapes of Wrath*.

It was August 1942. I am amazed that my parents left behind everything familiar and moved into a world they scarcely knew. They gambled everything on a belief that anytime could be good for new beginnings, *if* a person moved ahead with faith fixed in God.

Thankfully, they found a better life in California. A small Church of the Nazarene pastored by Rev. Frank Watkins became our place of worship. My father and mother both worked in new vocations until we began to overcome the haunting poverty. They were godly examples before their large family. One by one, members of the family, including myself, placed our own faith in their God. An amazing legacy comprised of four generations now follows in the trail of my parents. More than 100 of these attended the funeral celebrations for my father and later for my mother. Almost every one of that legacy claims the faith so vividly portrayed by my parents.

In my teen years I answered God's call to pastoral ministry. I completed the formal training and took my bride from the Nazarene parsonage home of her parents, L. I. and Opal Weaver, where she had received her own godly heritage, to our first church—a small home mission endeavor. The tiny nucleus of people had converted a garage into a small house where we would live. (We often questioned the authenticity of that structure's "conversion" experience!) There we began 25 years of pastoral ministry that spanned four different and wonderful congregations.

As He did for my parents, God also brought new beginnings into our lives. We found again and again that the safest place in the world is in the center of God's will.

One new beginning was an 11-year period in the district superintendency with a great family of Nazarene churches on the Southern California District.

From there, God's plan led surprisingly into a global assignment directing World Mission for the Nazarene denomination. Wonderful missionaries became our parishioners, and with them, we saw God's power at work in more than 100 countries. Visiting more than 90 of those countries was inconceivable for a Texas dust bowl farm boy to imagine!

During those days, dramatic changes occurred in East Europe and Asia and Africa. Political structures were discarded and new systems of life sought. I saw the Berlin Wall fall. I sat in government offices of Russia, Albania, Vietnam, and others and negotiated arrangements to send Christian missionaries into countries that now hoped for better days. It was an exhilarating time to be alive and a thrilling task in which to be engaged. Watching God work in those countries, making new converts, and building new churches out of the rubble of the past, I learned again: *Anytime is a good and possible time for new beginnings with God.*

In early 1994, I was asked to develop a 21st-century research institute that would seek strategies for greater church effectiveness in the postmodern world. I struggled with the decision. Did I want to leave the beloved missions work? Was it wise to enter a new, somewhat nebulous vocation at this time in my life?

My son, Steve, a Nazarene pastor, offered a pastoral word. "If you do it, Dad," he said, "don't do it only as an administrative task. Do it for Heather and Holly, Robert and David (my four grandchildren). Do it to help provide their new century with the best possible world and a better church than they might otherwise have."

I accepted the new assignment with that driving force. "Help design a new day and a church with God-beginnings in them." Across four years of intensive research, I've studied hundreds of books about the new century, analyzing emerging technology, culture, globalization, and economics. We interviewed leaders of more than 25 denominations and religious organizations. We talked with educators and politicians from local communities to the United Nations, considering global views and issues.

Repeatedly we addressed, "How will the dramatic courses of the emerging world be negotiated? In a cyber age of exploding knowledge and change, can we identify and embrace wisdom that will bring us to a future we will want to live with? Do we have hope?" That was the heavy background question. "In a 21st-century world, can God's people experience and communicate hope, which is the common object of search in all of history and the world?"

The years of research and study took me across North America, and again around the world. Out of such experiences I observed over and over that our God specializes in giving new beginnings. I have talked to hundreds, perhaps thousands, of people making new beginnings with God in their lives, their homes, their churches. Now they face the future unafraid. I have worshiped with and led seminars for scores of North American churches who are freshly discovering God's power. They are becoming God's beacons of hope in the quickly changing world.

I'm thankful for these experiences. I'm glad I learned to walk through sometimes frightening "open doors," though each contained its own painful changes. The years and experiences have confirmed that when we put God's will first, and focus God's face within the picture, life offers meaning through any change. With exhilaration, I approached my three-score years and ten, fully believing that God's continuing chapters for my life will be as fulfilling as those behind.

My life-proven conviction is: *with God, the best is always yet to be.* He supplies more than endurance and gives more than survival. He enhances life with optimism and productivity. With Him, meaningful discoveries are always arising. And any dedicated person can make a meaningful contribution to the future. I feel the significance of a Native American Indian saying. "We have not inherited the earth from our fathers. We are borrowing it from our children." Someday, perhaps sooner than I realize, I must hand the world to my children and grandchildren. My daily passion is that because of the stewardship of my life, it will be a better world.

So, new beginnings are not just for the century or millennium. Any person or church can make them if only we trust and obey!

Marriages and families can find wonderful new beginnings. A superior court judge told of his failed marriage. One day the stress became so great he left the bench, retired to his chambers, silently staring at rows of books. He noticed a black book on one of the shelves, stiff from not having been opened for a long time. It was a Bible. He took it from the shelf and thumbed its pages. He implored the power and person of this book to help him in his personal distress. God answered that prayer, and the distinguished judge's life began to turn around, carrying over into his troubled marriage. "My wife and I discovered we were able to begin loving each other all over again." Their hopeless despair dawned in a beautiful new beginning.

Those who once followed Christ but drifted away can also experience new beginnings. New spiritual romance awaits those trapped in spiritual apathy. The unfulfilling present need not be a permanent prison. God's promise to Israel in its trouble-filled day touches every troubled 21st-century life. "'Return, faithless Israel,' declares the LORD, 'I will frown on you no longer, for I am merciful,' declares the LORD, 'I will not be angry forever. Only acknowledge your guilt'" (Jer. 3:12-13). A new beginning can lead to a hope-filled future.

Churches can make new beginnings. One of the great old "First Churches" of the United States was down to 31 people after an illustrious history. A young pastor accepted its responsibility, eliminating such words as *failure* and *closure* from his vocabulary. Through prayer, example, dedication, and loving evangelism, he led the tiny remnant of people into a new day of ministry and spiritual impact. New beginnings are never beyond reach.

In every case, new beginnings take courage. They require facing realities and new prices of commitment. They require a willingness to go beyond a good beginning. The hunger for a better future must be nurtured. An ongoing quest for God's will must be present. But the new beginning can be made, and a new future can unfold.

God desires this more than we do. And He is safe to follow. With His will as our focus and His Holy Spirit as our Guide, any time is a great time for new beginnings. That is what sovereignty and grace are all about.

The future. It's here. So what? Grace-giving, sovereign God has a wonderful plan for you. It's new beginnings time!

PART 3

■

It's Here—Now What?

The hardest thing to convey in writing history is that nothing ever had to happen the way it happened.
—David McCullough

Although they [ships] are so large and are driven by strong winds, they are steered by a very small rudder wherever the pilot wants to go.
—James 3:4

If we could first know where we are, and whither we are tending, we could better judge what to do, and how to do it.
—Abraham Lincoln

■

Dialogue in Real Time

Hello again, A.D. 2001-plus. Here's the really big question: Will things get better or worse? Can we even know? And, can anyone make a lasting difference to better the available scenarios? Especially, can one ordinary person make a difference?

You see, A.D. 2001-plus, these are a few of the big questions you've evoked.

We know the jury is still out on the answers. As to what might be possible, God has left no doubt about His plan. Linked with Him, the people of a 3rd millennium or even a 10th millennium can become what their day needs most. Yeast that penetrates culture. Light that illuminates a direction of hope in the darkness. Salt that adds winsome favor. That's the promise of our grace-giving God. History's lessons prove it can happen. As always, His followers play a key role.

10

You Can't Predict but You Can Invent the Future. How?

WALTER LORD once wrote *The Good Years* about the era encompassing the beginning of the 20th century to the First World War in North American history. He pointed out that in many nations these were years of privilege, peace, and prosperity. Nevertheless, these years held many contradictions and various life qualities. What made the years good, according to the author, was something besides positive external conditions. Though rich men rode in private railroad cars and gave magnificent parties, this did not make the years good. Most people rarely traveled and went to no parties.

Though the world was at peace, this did not make the years good. Even in this peace time, millions of Americans were victims of oppressive imperialisms. Nor were these good years because costs of living were low—you could buy a shirt for only 23 cents, but it was a product of child labor.

Within such gross disparities, however, Walter Lord found something he believed made these years deserve being called "good." A unique kind of resistance was rising within the citizenry. People nurtured a conviction that life could be better. They energetically committed themselves to fixing the problems that existed.

Actually, many solutions were offered. They differed dramatically, and many people could hardly wait to test their proposals. This mind-set brought progress. Walter

Lord believed such sincere effort deserved commendation. He therefore titled his book and these years, _Good Years._ Their confidence, buoyancy, and spirit deserved to be called good. When people confront challenging realities with strong resolve and constructive experimentation that brings improvement, that time deserves to be called good.[1]

Now we face a day with new and complex problems. Thankfully, this century has brought a plethora of amazing privileges, prosperity, and international peace. Yet no one can fail to see or feel the dark pathologies lurking in its upbeat conditions. How should we think of a time like this? If we can find spirits of resolve and resilience, can we call these years good?

Each of us will formulate our own answer, hopefully using carefully chosen criteria. We stand at a significant fork in the road. We have reached what Aleksandr Solzhenitsyn called in his Harvard commencement address, "a watershed in history, equal in importance to the turn from the Middle Ages to the Renaissance. It will demand from us a spiritual blaze. We shall have to rise to a new height of vision, to a new level of life, where our physical nature will not be cursed, as in the Middle Ages, but even more importantly, where our spiritual being will not be trampled upon, as in the Modern Era."

If we navigate these years with this mind-set, they may become good years. If we fail to do so, we will travel roads that may lead to incomprehensible disasters.

The future. It's here. Now what? The question requires honest deliberation. What issues should concern us most? Which should we confront first? What alternative patterns should we consider? What steps should we take to get from where we are to where we need to be?

Through years of working with people around the world, I have observed that most are willing to do the right thing. Unfortunately we face confusion about what specifically to do, and how to do it.

In the late 20th century, a new science rose to prominence in academies of learning. Anticipating millennium change, scientists grew interested in how life and culture would evolve in the future, resulting in the science of future studies. Future studies is now an academically respected discipline, with its students studying social trends, exploring projections, and advocating actions to improve the future. Making no claim to *predict* the future, it fosters the belief that a better future can, however, be *invented.*

The science of future studies counsels people or institutions wishing to thrive in tomorrow's high-tech world, to reject a "business as usual" philosophy. Taking a hard look at culture evolutions, we must embrace a quest for learning. We must try to see where and why today's realities are designed, by whom, and how such forces are driven. Given the changing nature of today's world, we need to take decisive actions. This is the futurist's work.

I am challenged with the thought of being a *Christian futurist.* This might be the worthy aspiration of any person who believes in God and in His plan for this world. Christian futurists will imagine the future that would result from God's best plan at work, and then engage processes that help bring it to pass. This must be more than fantasies. Those who believe in God will begin from faith and conviction that the "earthen vessel" and "mustard seed" of their lives can become God's instrument. Wherever circumstances of life have placed them, however complex the issues or inadequate the resources, they will resist the temptation to panic. They will believe that God will make a way where none seems to exist. Such action makes them God's partners to help His kingdom come, His will be done on earth as it is in heaven.

Years ago social scientist Arnold Mitchell exhorted his colleagues to better the future socially. His challenge has pertinent application for people of faith. "It is essential," he said, "to live in the way you think the world should be. If voluntary simplicity is your vision of the ideal society, you should live the simple life. By *being* what you *believe* —a task of supreme difficulty—you become a *living advertisement* for the kind of future you believe in. In the long run, this may be the most effective of all ways of shaping the future" (italics mine).[2]

The science of future studies proposes specific action principles to facilitate the invention of the future. These have application possibilities for us.

1. To invent a better future, we reject the assumptions that the future can't change or be improved. I ask myself as a Christian futurist, will I dare to believe that even *my* future, or that of my family, my church, my community, can be improved? Faith means I will believe in a better possibility even though it may not seem visible or possible at this moment. I can consider other circumstances in which God has accomplished great things despite apparent hopelessness. If God could reach through Old Testament Job's tragedy, or a modern-day superior court judge's tragedy, or a once-strong-now-dying old First Church tragedy, He can work in my circumstance.

The Old Testament gives us powerful encouragement in Lam. 3, "I am the man who has seen affliction by the rod of his wrath. . . . He has made me dwell in darkness like those long dead. . . . I have been deprived of peace . . . I say, 'My splendor is gone'" (vv. 1, 6, 17-18). Then God enabled that writer to reach deep within his troubled heart where he found the courage to add, "Yet this I call to mind and therefore I have hope: Because of the LORD's great love we are not consumed, for his compassions never fail. They are new every morning; great is your faithfulness" (vv. 21-22).

Chaos may have sapped the best of your hope and resilience. But dare to verbalize a better dream, and to pray, "I believe, help Thou my unbelief." Your own "nights" of despair can turn into "new morning" discoveries that enable you to sing, "Great is thy faithfulness, Lord, unto me." Prayer and contemplation on God's value systems give birth to new personal hope, and to visions of expanded possibility in the mission of our lives.

The future. It's here. So what? Though we cannot *predict* the future, we can *invent* a better one. A first step in doing so is to reject the assumption that the future cannot be changed and improved.

2. To invent a better future, the science of future studies counsels taking time to study and understand present realities and environments. Ask the question, "What ideas or moods or trends drive my situation? What will probably happen if things continue as they are?"

An old Chinese proverb says, "If we don't change the

direction we are going, we will likely end up where we are headed." If we extrapolate existing attitudes, dynamics, trends, and statistical realities, where will they take us, and what will the future look like?

Our culture has distinct patterns. How has life around us changed, and what effect do these changes have on my concerns, my family, my church, and my community? How do social change, demographics, economics, entertainment, and media expressions impact who I am, what my family is, what my church does, how schools educate students, and how my government responds? Can my church reach beyond past achievements and present constituents? Does my community feel any impact from my church?

Honest introspection is never easy. Someone has observed, "We don't see things as *they* are, we see them as *we* are." That's not good enough. We have to see things in their potential power and impact. American president Grover Cleveland observed, "It isn't that people can't see the solution. They can't see the problem."

Too much is at stake in our cyber world of pluralism and relativism for moral people to live in a twilight of understanding. Though the future cannot be predicted, it can be invented, and the right invention will only come from honest, ongoing assessments that identify where we are and where we will end up if we do not act with integrity and faith.

The future. It's here. Now what? We need to study and understand present realities. Of course, God will help us see and act responsibly as we invite His assistance and seek His will.

3. To invent the best possible future, the science of future studies admonishes that we specifically identify and articulate the most critical issues so we can effectively address them.

What are the most critical issues in your life? in your family? in your church? in your school? in your community? in the nation? in our world?

Over four years, those of us in the 21st-century research project, Reynolds Research Institute, talked extensively with church personnel at every level of the church. We asked, "What do *you* believe are this denomination's most critical issues as we enter the 21st century?"

From wide sources of concern, these leaders voiced an interesting consensus: Who and what will this denomination become in the 21st century? Will it be only a generic part of the world evangelical movement? Might it drift in directions that lose its denominational distinctives? Will it follow the path some other denominations have followed—being assimilated into culture and losing effectiveness because of spiritual compromise? Or will it maintain the course envisioned by founder Phineas Bresee, who called the denomination to confront its world with a compelling biblical message and holy lifestyle through expressions of social compassion, social concern, and social engagement?

It is encouraging that such a quality issue was expressed. The issue of identity has compelling correlation for individuals, for congregations, and for society in this future that has arrived.

This is, however, only one critical issue. Others to consider:

1. Will we deal credibly and realistically with inescapable change in our world?
2. Will we maintain distinction between what must be changed and what should not be changed?
3. Will we seek understanding and emotional growth so we can engage people around us in meaningful and constructive dialogue?
4. Will we model compassion, lead credibly, and advocate justice?
5. How will we deal with realities of economics, culture, technology, and political responsibility?
6. Will we model our lives from the example and teachings of Jesus Christ or from the world in which we live?

The future. It's here. Now what? May we carefully identify and articulate the most critical issues so we can effectively address them. Of course, our grace-giving, sovereign God will help us understand them as we seek His will.

4. To invent the best possible future, the science of future studies admonishes us to carefully identify our "reason for being," so this can become the guidepost of future energies.

Much has been written about the value of articulating a "mission statement"—what a person or group perceives their purpose to be. Such a statement determines which things receive most of our attention, energies, and financial investments.

Having a strong and worthy "sense of purpose" makes an enormous difference in how we handle the most crucial demands of life, as well as the nitty-gritty daily decisions, relationships, and responsibilities.

The future. It's here. Now what? May we credibly answer the question "Why are we here? What should my mission, or our mission be in a world like this 21st century?" Surely our God will guide us to a meaningful response.

5. To invent the best possible future, the science of future studies admonishes us to imagine how the chosen "purpose" will look as it is carried out.

If I feel strongly about why I am here, why this family, this church, this school exists, then I can construct "models" that portray how that purpose looks as, with God's help, it is fleshed out. The model is more than a static image of what might be ahead. The model is the dream, the goal, and the purpose moving into fruition.

"Simulation" is an interesting exercise in today's dynamic world. In the game Monopoly, the real estate market is simulated so players can experience the possibility and perils in property acquisition and sales. Military trainers conduct war games that simulate possible happenings so trainees can practice how best to confront potential perils. The computer world takes us to new levels of simulation.

Taking a purpose statement, or "reason for being," in hand, we can build models that show how the future might look if that mission is carried out. Contemplating the model helps facilitate specific steps we need to take, and prepare accountability provisions so the future unfolds as it should.

The future. It's here. Now what? May we carefully imagine how our purpose will look as it unfolds. Of course, God will help us project our vision with faith and hope and love.

6. Finally, the science of future studies reminds us we must implement our dream and mission by engaging in competent action.

Ironically, at this obvious point so many people and organizations fall short. Years ago I read a humorous aphorism attributed to Petronius Arbiter in A.D. 66:

> We trained hard—but it seemed that every time we were beginning to be formed up into teams, we would be reorganized. I was to learn later in life that we tend to meet any new situation by reorganizing. And, a wonderful method it can be for creating an illusion of progress while producing confusion, inefficiency, and demoralization.

He was bemoaning that state that remains in a never-ending exercise of "getting ready to live."

Paul identified one characteristic of "last days" as a time when people would be "always learning but never able to acknowledge the truth" (2 Tim. 3:7). He speaks of a state of existence in which people are curious about truth but never let the truth drive and manage life.

That is especially a trait of the 21st century. People talk extensively but do little. School grades falter because students don't do the work. Marriages fail because partners won't build the relationship. Workers lose jobs because they are lazy or distracted. Churches die because parishioners do not complete assignments and commitments. And government disintegrates while politicians proclaim their rhetoric and leave action unfinished in committee rooms. Will the epitaph of 21st-century society be: "They talked, but they never got around to *doing* the right thing!"

The best future is not a gift. It is a result of action and discipline and achievement. Eleanor Roosevelt said, "The future belongs to those who believe in the beauty of their dreams." It's true, but it is not enough. The future belongs to those who believe so strongly in their dreams that they will invest personal time, energy, soul, resources, and sacrifice into getting the job done.

To bring positive moral influence on our culture, and improve that culture through effective churches and congregations, we must implement a solid marriage of *doing* and *being*.

Church influence in the earlier 20th century was damaged by the absence of one or both of these qualities. An industrial age placed strong emphasis on the value of formulas and mechanical things, external and self-accomplished. America and the world believed in hard work, "We can fix it ourselves!" Often that hard work was a substitute for ethical consistency. Some people loudly professed spiritual belief and practiced certain church activities (attendance, office holding) while living with amazing inconsistencies in areas of ethics or expressions of Jesus' love. At best their love was harsh, and too often it was absent. People considered themselves holy because they did not dance, drink, smoke, or go to movies. They attended church and prayer meeting. Sadly, however, they indulged in gossip, judged others, and gave less than true stewardship expressions to God.

Understandably the children in such homes, the younger baby boomer generation and generation Xers, felt spiritual nausea at such aberrations. In bitterness about such inconsistencies, many left the church of their roots, changed denominations, or abandoned religion.

As our present time further exposes the fallacy of those former practices, what will we do about it? Will Christians and churches in the 21st-century world revert to the weakness of the former culture and sacrifice this moment of opportunity on the altar of inaction or inconsistency?

Surprisingly, in today's broad religious culture, we see a refreshing acknowledgment that *holiness* is indeed a word from God's vocabulary. Carried out in human life it means "wholeness"—not extremism, not radicalism, not ugliness. With beauty and healing, we're seeing the holy life as the ultimate answer to holistic hungers of the new generations. Many denominations, parachurch movements, and interdenominational movements are proclaiming the Holy Spirit and the Spirit-filled life. The age-old God-plan with its possibilities of transforming beauty is seen for what it is supposed to be: the only lasting answer to tragic life addictions, to disintegrating homes and families, to social maladies. The church movement that biblically teaches people how to be whole/holy in a chaotic cyber age will have a following. This is the marriage of biblical *being* and *doing* at its best.

The Church of the Nazarene has historic credentials identifying it with such mission. Strong recommitment to that heritage will give our denomination its best thrust into the third millennium. If we fail to do this, God will convey His message through other sources. Perhaps our grace-giving, sovereign God gave this denomination its first 100 years to work through petty distractions that were such a part of the modernity era. Now, 100 years later God longs to honor this church or any movement that will honor His plan of holy people loving holy God with heart, soul, mind, and strength. To *be* holy and to *do* holiness will invent the best future for person, marriage, family, church, and society.

The future. It's here. Now what? From such an academic discipline as the science of future studies, we are reminded that we must implement our mission with competent and continuing action. God invites us to a marriage of *being* and *doing* that will be the best of all gifts we can give as our legacy to the third millennium. He joins us at the "marriage" altar to recite His own special vow:

> "I know the plans I have for you," declares the LORD, "plans to prosper you and not to harm you, plans to give you hope and a future. Then you will call upon me and come and pray to me, and I will listen to you. You will seek me and find me when you seek me with all your heart. I will be found by you," declares the LORD, "and will bring you back from captivity" *(Jer. 29:11-14).*

11

People of the New Century: Who Are They?

AROUND THE CORNER from our Overland Park, Kansas, home lived a couple from a Middle Eastern country. They wore clothing of their former culture and practiced the Muslim faith. It was striking to see them, she with face covered, walking our neighborhood streets. Another person from their country became a cashier at the local Wal-Mart. She was typically Arabic in her dress but typically Wal-Mart in her courtesy.

Three blocks in another direction lived a couple from India. They, too, retained aspects of their Indian culture and were devout Hindus. I enjoyed chatting with them. They acknowledged it was not easy to transition from their former home to the Midwest. I understood that—I had visited India several times.

Visiting a Northern California town, I went to the front desk of my motel to ask a routine question. I was surprised to hear the clerk respond, "Lo siento, no hablo Ingles." *(I'm sorry, I do not speak English.)* In visits to Mexico City, Guatemala City, Managua, Nicaragua, Caracas, Venezuela, and many other Spanish-speaking countries, I had never encountered a lack of bilingual capability by hotel personnel. But here it was in the United States.

The future. It's here! Twenty-first century cyber age. And it has brought distinct "people changes" that no one can fail to observe.

Once-familiar communities have gone from single-family farms or homes with neighborly familiarity into sundry global and socially diverse communities. We see less people around us who are "people like *us*" (whoever *we* are). Instead, we see faces and sounds of people who are very *different* from us.

Who are the people of this new century we have entered?

The most obvious new faces in this future that has now arrived reveal a changing ethnicity, as reflected by my former Kansas neighbors.

This diversification is happening in many countries. Our planet has become a global village. One in 10 Americans were born in another country—most in Latin America and Asia. This is the highest proportion of non-U.S.-born citizens in the history of this nation.

Studies project that people of Latin country origins will be the largest minority group in the United States early in the 21st century. People of Asian country origins represent the most rapidly growing group. And children of mixed marriages may be the fastest growing minority group in North America. As long ago as 1989, futurist Tom Sine suggested that young people who could communicate in only one language and were raised in nearly all white American suburbs would be culturally disadvantaged in the 1990s. "They will be ill-equipped to participate in the increasingly cross-cultural and transnational environment of tomorrow's world."[1] Time is proving him right.

Who are the people of this new century? How will we understand or communicate with each other?

The social landscape changes are more than just those of ethnic pluralization. New faces bring dramatically different lifestyles and philosophies—different values, attitudes, and alliances. They constitute a less visibly obvious, though far more socially alarming component than those who speak another language. Their faces reflect the reality and rise of secular and cultural humanism.

Secular and cultural humanism is the lifestyle of people who structure their lives outside of the Judeo-Christian culture. The number of such people is exploding in America and around the world. Judeo-Christian principles were once dominant, especially in Western civilization. That fact has changed.

Dr. George Hunter of Asbury Seminary notes that the average Sunday church attendance has declined to 6 percent in West Germany and Italy, to between 1 and 3 percent in the Scandinavian countries, to 12 percent in Great Britain. In Canada it is less than half of what it was 40 years ago. In Australia it is less than half of what it was 25 years ago.

In the United States the figure has consistently been less than 40 percent for several years. The United States has what Dr. Hunter calls at least 120 million functionally undiscipled people.[2] George Gallup also notes the growth in numbers and influence of humanists. Gallup calls these "people with no Christian memory."

The influence of this cultural diversification significantly affects our future. Within present conditions, in newly emerging trends, and in yet to be born realities, are powerful magnitudes of potential impact on the world of century 21. All sorts of dramatic differences are imminent.

How could this happen? Where did it all begin? What drives its forcefulness?

People of faith in God and of strong belief in His "lessons of history" recognize in humanism a continuation of the age-old problem of sin. When Adam and Eve chose self-will over obedience to their Creator-God, the door opened for myriad shapes and sorts of human evil and desperation to unfold. The creativity of sin and the ingenuity of Satan never cease to amaze us. Evil and injustice capitalize on every avenue imaginable to explode and pollute people and nations.

Sadly, much of this happens through channels of government leadership and is perpetrated by leaders who abuse the public trust. During his second term of office, President Bill Clinton appointed more than 170 federal judges, constituting 70 percent of this nation's judiciary. The appointment pattern showed a steady selection of people who had distinct bias against strong moral and spiritual commitments and wished to rewrite law with secular sympathies instead of interpreting laws as established by the nation's founders.

Writing on the effect of this travesty in political leadership, U.S. Supreme Court Justice Antonin Scalia wrote, "Case by case, the courts are busy designing a Constitution for a country I do not recognize."[3]

Rulings are repeatedly given, lobbied by such organizations as the American Civil Liberties Union, which are hostile toward traditions of religious and moral principle. It will be years before our secular judiciary, appointed for life, ceases to be a dangerous power, because most of the current judiciary's rulings hinder civility or liberty.

Today's powerful entertainment and media industries are two other massive forces that boldly assist humanism and accelerate departure from Judeo-Christian influence. The Time-Warner Corporation is one of the worst offenders. Some estimate it to be the world's most powerful industry in the field of communication. In 1995, *Newsweek* magazine called Time-Warner the corporation doing more than any other to degrade the American culture.

With all these influences, the populace of the secular humanists continues to explode with increasingly influential voices.

The future. It's here. Now what? It's here with people speaking new "languages" of linguistic and culture values.

As we know these people better, we will face a sobering question: What can believers, people with only "mustard seed" proportions, do about this reality?

The answer is not simple, but neither is it complex enough to bury us in hopelessness. In fact, it is much more reachable than we probably realize.

All people of all centuries and all nations and all cultures of the world are the outflow of God's creative hand. We know this from the creation story of God's Word and the evidences of history. The Creator-God implanted a God-shaped vacuum within His creation that no person of any race or language or economy or culture or aberration can escape.

We can easily forget that as we encounter people with so many different languages, cultures, value systems, or ideology. Therefore authentic Christians need a reality check, and a response change.

May we more carefully consider such statements as one by Richard Slaughter, director of the Future Study Centre in Melbourne, Australia. He wrote, "There is a spiritual vacuum at the heart of industrialized culture which makes it very difficult for people to resolve the perennial concerns of human existence."

He points out that our world offers many substitute satisfactions. But at deep levels, people are not fooled. Their needs cannot be met without a spiritually correct discovery.[4] The Bible clearly teaches that answer is found in knowing, loving, and serving Jesus Christ.

Can a person of dramatically different ethnic origin or of cultural humanism find such knowledge? Of course! Around the world, I have visited with people coming out of every conceivable world religion. I have heard them confess the joy of Jesus Christ over their former beliefs. With respect to those in the Western world's cultural humanism, we can hear grateful voices from every part of the nation affirming their deliverance in Jesus Christ.

We don't need to cleverly compose arguments or strategies or have sophisticated understanding and minds to win such lives. Something happens when we live a simple, contagious life before others. Something happens when we live with consistent integrity and lovingness. Such genuineness impacts unbelievers and draws out their admission of their hunger and need.

The components that win people of the new century world are simple. We must begin with people where they are. We must develop credibility by being good listeners, and not returning arguments. We must speak with them in a language they can understand linguistically and culturally—without religious clichés. We must present a Christianity that positively addresses the pressing issues of their lives and of ours. We must approach them with what George Hunter calls "Christianity 101." Keep it simple! Realize that effective evangelism may be a process that takes awhile.

Most of all, we must remember that it is not our words or knowledge or cleverness or forcefulness that ultimately compels people to change. It is Jesus Christ, working through us.

A wonderful young family moved next door to us. They were materially secure and socially engaged in work and friendship. Church was not part of their lives. But they were also human, with problems like most people know well. For five years my wife, Carolyn, and I loved them, talked to them, ate meals with them, and prayed for them. Then we received a Saturday night phone call: "Can we go to church with you tomorrow?"

That Sunday our pastor covered every possible deviant area of life. Though he did so in a spirit of love, we held our breath. Would it be too much too soon for people who are new to such thoughts? After the service, however, their response confirmed how God's gracious Spirit was engaging them. They said, "You know, everything he said was true. Those things are ripping our lives apart."

We kept loving them. Three months later they walked the church aisle to an altar of prayer. A few months later they took vows of church membership. What a change. And they still thank God for the hope He implanted in their lives.

Take time with the people you know. You have the privilege to love them. You do not have to change them or save them. Only God can do that. And His ways to do that may surprise you. Give Him, and them, time. Just be nice.

I believe one of the most powerful tools a believer may use to bring friends, family, and newcomers to Jesus Christ is this: *Just be nice.* Redemptive "niceness" has its own special content. It means:

—— **N**otice me
—— (Take an) **I**nterest in me
—— **C**onnect with me
—— **E**nnoble me

In a world of crudity, cruelty, and detachment, the power of being nice is one of the most powerful responses we can offer.

The future. It's here. Now what?

Who are the people of a new century? Coming from such diverse backgrounds, can they have interest in the Jesus I know? Can I become an instrument in the process of creating a new future for them? Our grace-giving, sovereign God can take what we give Him in our mustard-seed limitations and make us yeast and light and salt until they come back home. It can happen.

> *Down in the human heart, crushed by the tempter,*
> *Feelings lie buried that grace can restore.*
> *Touched by a loving heart, wakened by kindness,*
> *Chords that are broken will vibrate once more.*

12

Programs Aren't Forever, but Principles Can Be

THE FUTURE. It's here. Now what?

Part of the peril in today's enamored practice with paradigm shifts is that every new paradigm is assumed to overthrow and better what came before, starting from scratch. Virginia Postrel, in *The Future and Its Enemies,* suggests that we actually have no "scratch" to start from. History is real, and therefore progress comes only from proper respect for and learning from past experiences. We should neither forget, nor cease being grateful, for enrichments that may have come from a very different past. It is true, however, that in retrospect we can more easily see the flaws.

Flashing back to the home page of the early 20th century, we discover an exploding world, similar to that of century 21. In the February 2000 edition of *Harper Management Update,* the editor reminded readers that today's pace of change has not been too different from the early 20th century. The first factory powered by electricity was built in 1894. By 1901 nearly 400,000 electric motors drove industrial machinery. The number of electrical generating plants grew from 1 to 2,000 in 20 years. Street-railway mileage rose from near zero to 22,000. The early 20th century saw new realities of radio, air travel, electricity, telephones, movies, and automobiles.

In *Our Times,* Mark Sullivan and Dan Rather remind us that newspapers of January 1, 1900, did not carry words such as *radio, aviator, insulin,* or *tractors.* Between 1900 and 1925 dictionaries added thousands of new words to accommodate the explosions in a complex civilization.[1]

Sullivan and Rather note the rapidity of change and how important it was for people to keep an open mind:

> Perhaps it is just as well the schoolchildren did not learn much of what science thought it knew in the 1870s and 1880s. . . . They would have known a good deal that was not so, would have had their minds set against the amazing revelations that science was bringing about. It was difficult for some who followed science as a career to adjust their minds to the changes.[2]

We do not know how much we will have to get rid of in what we think we know today, and how much new "knowledge" may contain serious flaws.

In looking at the past, we can see how the world was increasingly enamored in thought patterns that were problematical before the century ended. Celebrating modernism and industrialism, many believed scientific formula and programmed developments could resolve human need. Even as wars broke out and materialism fluctuated, such beliefs persisted. Some felt they could solve life's problems with better job descriptions, with more careful management, by understanding and practicing reengineering, by adding more power to machinery, by building more modern industrial complexes, by exploiting scientific possibilities.

Church bureaucracies did not escape this thinking. Churches could grow, people believed, if organizational aspects improved, if programs expanded, if activities increased, and if promotional tools were used. Religious communities received pressure to try harder, do more, set bigger goals, improve structures, and raise more money. The most intense efforts were rewarded, implying these were the way to achievement and spiritual fulfillment. A congregation was applauded when it increased its numbers and income—for visible results.

But just as the world did not achieve peace by possessing bigger weapons, the 20th century revealed that programs alone did not bring personal growth, permanent church growth, or Christian impact on society.

In the clutter of this "dance with doing" we lost the value of the "being" quality with the "doing" urgency. Modernity and industrialization placed their bets on doing. Although the Bible denied that salvation could come by works, people still tried to make church grow by bigger and better program efforts.

Late 20th-century protests exposed the over-drawn claims of modernism and industrialization and brought us into the postmodernism mind-set. Though it has weaknesses, we can hope in this new era we will have a better perspective on modernity's limitations and on the powers needed beyond these. We need to give priority again to life structured not around programs and power, but around purpose and principles. Programs do not last forever, but principles can.

As I have observed people and churches around the world in recent years, I've seen that many still focus on programs. It is also refreshingly obvious which ones operate by principles.

Generally, people obsessed with programs lack resiliency and creativity. Parenting programs alone do not make children perfect or reduce the frustration of hopeful parents. Excellent counseling programs alone cannot make congregations or individuals well-balanced or harmonious people. Sunday School contests do not automatically bring quality growth for church congregations. Efficient bureaucracies do not always help denominations reach their world for Christ. Even some professing Christians who boast of following church-defined programs may not influence those around them. Programs are not enough.

On the other hand, I have noted individuals and congregations who prioritized principles over programs. They did have programs, but the programs grew out of principles. These people or groups did not emphasize growth, but health. Health will result in growth, but growth does not always result in health.

Excellent books have been written that may help us develop principles, such as Dennis Kinlaw's book *The*

Mind of Christ, and Christian Schwarz's book *Natural Church Development: A Guide to Essential Qualities of Healthy Churches.*[3]

While studying Christians and churches that are significantly impacting their culture, I have noted 14 principles often present:

1. Effective, healthy believers or churches focus life carefully around God's Word.

What counts most is what God's Word says. Following the Bible is neither mechanical nor morose. It is the object of disciplined study, contemporary understanding, and application. Jesus said, "If you hold to my teaching, you are really my disciples. Then you will know the truth, and the truth will set you free" (John 8:31-32). *The Jerusalem Bible* translates Jesus' words, "If you make my word your home, you will indeed be my disciples, you will learn the truth and the truth will make you free."

2. Effective, healthy believers biblically answer the question "Who am I?" or "Who are we?"

As they find their identity in Christ, they find significance and esteem. They understand the difference between carnal pride and humility and sanctified pride and humility. They live celebration lives of obedience and freedom. With conviction that they are God's children, they can live in obedience and freedom, in lives of celebration and stability.

3. Effective, healthy believers and churches honestly ask, "Where am I?"

They insist on knowing their community and world and on being realistic and redemptive. They do not live in yesterday or in a make-believe world. They embrace people and circumstances around them and love without prejudice or exclusiveness.

4. Effective, healthy believers and churches have strong convictions about "Why am I here?"

This is the issue of vision and mission. The purpose of life or church is first of all to glorify God. The next purpose is to bring other people to Jesus Christ. Tom Sine observes, "Most churches are afflicted with chronic randomness." But healthy, effective people and churches are driven by compelling vision, a strong sense of purpose, and a consistently executed mission.

5. Effective, healthy believers and congregations are concerned about how they are perceived.

Though they are not controlled by image or opinions, they are sensitive to people. None of us will win someone to our belief system or friendship circle without courtesy, authenticity, and sensitivity to others' thoughts and needs.

6. Effective, healthy believers and congregations correctly define and consistently practice authentic worship.

Worship is more than a style of discipline or music expression. Authentic worship is an experience of connection between the worshiper and God. That connection may be facilitated by a person's music or liturgy task. Healthy believers and congregations focus on a personal connection with God in worship, knowing that leads to a holy and healthy connection with people.

7. Effective, healthy believers cherish spiritual relationships with others.

Christian Schwarz's research found that small-group ministries are most frequently present in healthy, growing churches. As Christians in a secular world, we need accountability and communication with others of like faith to grow spiritually.

8. Effective, healthy believers and congregations carry out life and church activities in frameworks of functional creativity and flexibility.

Leonard Sweet admonishes, "In a world where the edges are getting softer, our core needs to be harder than ever."[4]

But as a core is sacredly maintained, life systems and functions must be creatively adapted. The mind-set of "We never did it that way before" is dropped from the vocabulary as systems remain flexible.

9. Effective, healthy believers and congregations live and thrive in a "servant" spirit.

Jesus dignified and modeled that concept. Being a servant is a matter of looking for ways to be nice and helpful. Visiting Mother Teresa's home in Calcutta, I saw this saying on her wall: "I don't do big things. I do small things with a big love." That's servanthood. It's a secret of effective people and congregations.

10. Effective, healthy believers and congregations are examples of concern and cooperation in their communities.

They are friendly, not withdrawn. They are observant, not disinterested. They are cooperators, not criticizers. They care about school and government efficiency. They are partners with other churches and community organizations. They want to be yeast and light and salt.

11. Effective, healthy believers are characterized by a biblical sense of family.

Family has become an empty word for many in this century's vocabulary. In the last 25 years, the number of people living alone has doubled, and the frequency of Americans having family dinner has declined 30 percent. More than a million children endure divorce every year. Our urgent mission as people of faith is to model "biblical" family, with its togetherness, respect, affirmations, helpfulness, and loving acceptance.

12. Effective, healthy believers and congregations expand the measuring systems by which they assess their effectiveness.

The age of modernity and industrialization measured results in visible numbers and quotients. Many people and churches still use such visible components to indicate progress. The biblical measuring system is far more than "how many now compared to last year." It is "What evidences of spiritual maturity can we see?" "How creatively do we connect with people?"

13. Effective, healthy believers live unintimidated by the phenomenon of change.

They understand they cannot avoid change. They seek to manage change so it serves rather than enslaves them and their purposes. They know that they can effectively change with time and prayer and transition.

14. Effective, healthy believers and congregations seek to be Spirit-directed in purpose and attitude and process.

When healthy growth is present, the person or community of faith knows the bottom line is the quality of relationship with God, and obedience. They constantly live in a natural atmosphere and discipline of prayer.

Jim Cymbala of Brooklyn Tabernacle pinpointed prayer as the turning point in his life and ministry. Bill Hybels attributes the impact of Willow Creek church to this: "We did not dream to be a big church," he says. "We dreamed how to be an Acts 2 fellowship."[5] This is consistent with the believers and healthy, growing congregations I have seen around the world. Principles such as these, not programs, are keys to healthy, growing believers and churches.

Modernity and industrialization missed a vital point. Though they brought many positive realities to life, their programs and bureaucracies and unions and schemes were not enough. We see this as we hyperlink with the home page of the 20th century and the human need of the 21st century. Solid principles are the hope and key. These will give birth to programs that will serve the best purposes but will be modified as circumstances require.

The future now here scarcely possesses a more urgent "now what?" *Programs are not enough,* because they do not last forever. But *principles* can last *forever.* As we partner with our grace-giving God, proven principles, practiced faith, and persistent obedience will make the future what it needs to be.

13

What It Looks Like: The Healthy "Tomorrow Church"

THE FUTURE. Its here. Now what? A healthy tomorrow church will exist!

Not all of tomorrow's healthy churches will look alike. Some will be hybrid. Some will be megachurches. Some will be tiny. Some will meet in million-dollar complexes. Some will meet in rented rooms. Some will operate from huge budgets with many paid staff and extensive resources. Others will barely exist from week to week, without a paid pastor. Some will be homogeneous groups of people. Others will be singular in culture. Some will be in rural settings, others in suburbs, and still others in dying downtown worlds.

We must remember that century 21 brings us into a world that is growing more dramatically diverse than any other century. The 21st century world will be a world of both/and, not either/or. This fact will be expressed in what healthy churches look like.

Whatever the tomorrow world throws at its emerging populace, and however that populace develops, an authentic church will be there. *Church* means "a group of called-out people"—people on God's mission. In all the passing varieties of time and history, God has never left himself without a witness. Nor will He. "I will put together my church," Jesus said, "a church so expansive with energy that not even the gates of hell will be able to keep it out" (Matt. 16:18, TM).

This has been confirmed in every era of history. At times it seemed His cause was silenced. The mustard seed was only dormant however, not dead. The springtime of a new day dawned, and the tiny green shoots appeared. He kept His church alive. He will always do that as part of His promise and plan. Until Jesus returns to bring the Kingdom's eternal order, He will keep "putting together His church and overwhelming hell" with His kingdom.

Whatever the wide expressions of that church may be, the healthy tomorrow church will contain certain common elements.

1. Strong identity and engagement with its community will characterize the church. It will be effective because of its integrity and mission focus.

2. It's clergy and lay leadership will maintain spiritual authenticity, by sensitivity to their community, by a redemptive engagement, by communication that connects with people, and by their passion and persistence. They will not base their qualification for ministry on educational achievements or impressive accomplishments or charm.

3. Congregation size or facility magnificence will not be the determining criteria for the healthy tomorrow church. Richard Foster suggests that our world has had too much of an edifice complex, and some have gone too far in trying to accomplish spiritual mission and issues with buildings. Doctrinal clarity and life examples bring people and God together. Buildings do not give birth to people. The third world house-church movements with lay leaders serving as clergy have seen the greatest explosions of evangelism and growth in the 20th century. Can this happen in the affluent Western world? It can, and it will.

Foster believes "megachurches are not the wave of the future." Such thinking is substantiated in unfolding economic realities and by unfolding political oppositions and social crosscurrents. Hopefully "superchurches" will continue to be viable forces, with more emerging. But God will not use just huge instruments to impact culture. Size and resource abundance are not the only channels He will work through. Foster points out, "We are in a spiritual centrifuge. Old densities are breaking up. Structures of new densities are not yet clear. This is a (moment of) great opportunity to see what God is doing, and move with Him."[1]

4. The clergy and laity of the healthy tomorrow church will make sure they are growing in mind, alive in heart, and relevant in their communities. They will emphasize lifelong learning. Healthy tomorrow churches will be bases of educational opportunity for their communities. They will offer adult courses at community levels, as well as life-improvement avenues for children and youth, those marrying, and families. Curriculum will address life needs and be consistent with biblical truth. Many congregations will offer English as a second language and classes to help immigrants enter Western society. Other congregations will offer computer and Internet training for those who need help to enter the cyber age.

As the baby boomer generation becomes the largest number of older people alive at any time in history, congregations will help boomers face advancing years with grace and usefulness, and through applying the Bible to life. They will also discover ways to incorporate this resource into new dimensions of stewardship. The healthy tomorrow church will be an important component in its community's learning base.

5. The healthy tomorrow church will develop relational networks that build positive bridges among various groups of people. It will be known for holistic expressions and convictions that accrue to the community good. It will be a model of inclusiveness, blending generations and ethnic groups, and economic groups. The healthy tomorrow church will have a vision for the entire world. It will compassionately embrace people, helping them discover truth in Jesus Christ.

6. The healthy tomorrow church will have fruit to reflect its engagements. It will not only be winsome but winning. It will be an instrument through which lives are born into the divine kingdom:

- where disenfranchised persons can recover their heritage in Jesus Christ
- where evil addictions are broken
- where marginalized people come into joy in God's family
- where children, youth, and adults find dignity and respect in better relationships with people and God

7. The ultimate validation, the most powerful cohesiveness, and the distinction of the healthy tomorrow church will be its unmistakable focus on others. It is clearly an agency that does God's business. It guards and expands its connection with our grace-giving, sovereign God. The healthy tomorrow church will reflect a positive, loving Divinity, who inspires trust, generates hope, renews peace, and elevates life without regard to caste, class, gender, or jurisdiction. What a valuable place this church will be for a confused, hurting world!

The future. It's here. Now what? Dream this dream for your congregation. Become part of such a spiritual family for your community. This is the embodiment of our sovereign God's dream, and He will help bring it to fruition.

14

Leadership's New Face: Guess Who It Looks Like. You!

THE FUTURE. It's here. Now what?

It's an almost universal agreement: One of the greatest needs in this new world is for *leadership.* We hear a desperate call for *leaders* who will help get us through the twisting, perilous canyons before us.

Contemplating this need we groan with wishful thoughts of "if only." If only the world had another Churchill. If only the nation had another Abraham Lincoln. If only society's hurts had another Florence Nightingale or Mother Teresa. If only our social prejudices had another Susan B. Anthony or Martin Luther King. If only the delicate issues between today's angry nations could be negotiated by the balanced mind of a Dag Hammarskjöld. If only today's church had another John Wesley, Phineas Bresee, or J. B. Chapman. If only . . .

We need visionary leadership in this "now what?" moment of the future. We need trustworthy statesmanship. We need skillful negotiators. We need insightful humanitarians. We need powerful communicators. We need creative minds. We need examples of integrity and courage. We need prophets.

Where are great leaders when we so badly need them? Where are the statesmen who can inspire right responses? Where are the heroes who model character? Where are intellectuals who will do more than replay yesterday's clichés? Where are the hard workers? Where are the socially sensitive who will not practice cronyism? Where are real men and women who will never sacrifice their leadership opportunity in gamesmanship, political aspiration, or self-centered role-playing? For a world in spiritual and moral darkness, where are those who will authentically pray and communicate with people?

The future is here. Now what? If only . . .

Young and old carry deep fears in this arrived future. What lies ahead? Will it be nuclear holocaust? or natural disaster from global warming? or bloodbath from a Bin Laden terrorist group? or loss of religious freedom through aggressiveness of humanists in Washington or secular media influence? or an Armageddon because of return to Sodom and Gomorrah led by the moral perverseness?

What's ahead? Will my marriage survive? Will my family hold together? Will my educational dream come true? Will my vocational plan succeed? Will my church be more than a wax museum of past glory? Will democracy survive?

What's ahead? It's scary, isn't it?

Is it beyond your wildest imagination that *you* might fill a leadership role in bringing about the best answers? We need leadership to get us through "this," whatever "this" is. And in God's ingenuity, the face of that leadership looks more familiar than we realize!

Few fields of human thought receive more attention today than the subject of leadership: assessing it, interpreting it, understanding it, reengineering it, wishing for it. As modernity has declined and postmodernism has risen, leadership's canvas is being repainted. Warren Bennis, distinguished University of Southern California professor and Leadership Institute chair, states: "We cling to the myth of the Lone Ranger, and tend to think of achievement in terms of the Great Man or Great Woman. . . . The more I look at the history of business, government, the arts, the sciences, the clearer it is that few great accomplishments are ever the work of a single [great] individual."

Bennis declares that "the Great *Group"* is now necessary. Today's organizations must determine how to get talented, self-absorbed, often arrogant, incredibly bright people to work together better. And Bennis adds, *"At the heart of every Great Group is a shared dream.*"[1] Luciano de Crescanzo paints an interesting word-picture: "We are angels with only one wing; we can only fly while embracing one another."

The 20th-century assumption was that leadership meant power personalities in control—generally the wealthy and visible. To succeed, an organization, nation, or group needed the "great leader." This assumption served well in the modernity and industrialization mind-set.

The 21st-century world, however, expects and demands a different concept for "leader." Peter Drucker points out that we are moving into a "network" society rather than one in which one strong personality carries all responsibility. We may still hope for gifted leaders. The 21st-century culture, however, is increasingly less responsive to autocracy of any kind. The 21st-century followers respond more to leadership that honors network dynamics.

Most of all, 21st-century leadership must model integrity and compassion. The new century leadership will help associates arrive at a collective mission understanding. The leaders' tones will lift the sights and spirits of those around them. The leaders will help others develop skills to produce a better tomorrow.

Leadership in the 21st-century world will work through conveners and clarifiers, through team players, through flexible and fluid management. It will celebrate the 1-talent person as well as the 10-talent person. Leadership in the 21st-century world will work through people of every age, education, and economic condition who will model right actions and love and serve others.

Churches need to surrender the notion that their pastor is the "actor" and they are "director" or "audience." Effective congregations will join their pastor to become the doers. God becomes the Director and the Audience.

"Leader" and "servant" will be fused to impact the 21st-century world. James O'Toole, vice president of the Aspen Institute, wrote a powerful book, *Leading Change.* This guru of the corporate world set Jesus Christ as the ideal model for leadership in a time of change. O'Toole believed Jesus established timeless evidence that the right kind of change cannot be commanded, just as the right kind of following cannot be forced. Nor did Jesus manipulate His followers. Jesus' leadership was a shepherding process. O'Toole believes it remains the greatest leadership example we have.[2]

I earlier suggested that *micro* and *macro* were two buzzwords of this new future. These buzzwords represent the minuscule and the massive dimensions of reality. Within the micro (the minuscule) is the intriguing world of nanotechnology and microtechnology. Their studies focus attention on the significant world of the atom. Some of today's most amazing accomplishments occur in this world that is often invisible to the naked eye. We are redesigning materials and structures using microscopic robots that manipulate individual atoms. Tiny "disease fighting submarines," for example, may one day circulate in a person's bloodstream to pursue harmful effects in the human body: fatty deposits, viruses, cancer cells, DNA mutations, and so forth. Others may regularly administer doses of medicine from inside the body.

No longer does the colossal, the visually powerful, the loud rule in shaping life's great marvels. We are acknowledging the significance of a nanotechnology world, the macro, the minuscule, the tiny.

This illustrates a powerful biblical truth. Jesus said, "The kingdom of heaven is like a mustard seed" (Matt. 13:31). Something as great and timeless as Kingdom business does not necessitate the super, the shrewd, the spectacular, the superlative, or even the splendid to win its world. God can use the simple, the small, and the ordinary—spiritual nanotechnology. The power of our gracegiving, sovereign God can accomplish surprising things through what the world would see as useless.

In 1994, I sat in the historic Government House of Hanoi, Vietnam, across the table from high government leaders. I had been invited to tell them about Nazarene global missions. It was one of the most electrifying moments of my career. Before me sat men of a Communist country that still had no official relation with many countries, including the United States. Imagine my astonishment to be greeted with, "Tell us about your church and how we might have people of your church come to work in our country." We spent two hours in an amazing discussion and came to a significant mutual agreement and made a unique arrangement unparalleled in other religious organizations of that time.

What brought about this stunning meeting? A wonderful Nazarene layman who was sitting beside me. He was a dark-skinned citizen from the South Pacific. He was in Vietnam to direct an economic recovery program administered by the United Nations. For months he had discreetly modeled his faith and told these leaders about his church. He reported how his church helped many nations through the message of Jesus Christ and His mission of love. They wanted to know more. I was there because of this unpretentious layman.

Two years before the Vietnam visit, this layman had been a United Nations director in Bangladesh. Through his work with government leaders there, the Church of the Nazarene was allowed to begin a ministry of compassion and evangelism in that nation. Today the church has an impressive presence in Bangladesh, led by strong national leaders. It started with this layman's influence.

The legacy now being written in Bangladesh and Vietnam began in a tiny South Pacific island country. Earlier in his life, this Nazarene layman was a successful businessman who knew nothing of the Church of the Nazarene. He had little time for church or God. At one point he began to build a home near a Nazarene church. A missionary's wife saw this man at the construction and wished to befriend the prospective occupants. She baked cookies, which her husband carried to the site. Busy as he was, this layman almost brushed off the missionary, but then, as he says, "I smelled the cookies."

The sweets captured his appetite and attention and were a starting point for a pleasant conversation. He accepted an invitation to visit the church. The promised visit turned to two, and then more. Some weeks later the businessman and his wife received Jesus Christ into their lives. They became faithful in that congregation and district. Then the United Nations summoned them to serve in distant countries. With them they took their faith and their love of the church.

Today, two nations of the world, Bangladesh and Vietnam, experience a growing influence of Jesus Christ and His church because of that layman's influence.

After leaving the government offices in Hanoi on that 1994 day, I enjoyed an evening with this churchman. Reflecting on the warm openness of those Vietnamese officials, and on what we knew was happening in Bangladesh, we praised God for His grace and sovereignty.

My host, the Nazarene layman of the small South Pacific island, the high official for United Nations Economic Recovery Programs for underdeveloped nations, said with a twinkle in his eye, "Not bad returns for the investment of a cookie."

The kingdom of heaven does indeed come through mustard-seed faith. In a world discovering nanotechnology, God continues His age-old practice, proving that little things do indeed mean much.

The Kingdom comes! It comes when Jesus' followers give away cookies, treat neighbors to a barbecue and Bible studies, cry with a coworker over a painful divorce, have patience with an addict, visit a nursing home, welcome a family from another country, chat with a child from the house next door, work behind the scenes, pray and love in His name. The Kingdom comes—by way of the mustard seed.

The future is here. Now what? It needs leadership. And the new faces of leadership may be people that a highly structured world might have overlooked. The faces of leadership in a new century include your face.

No, you do not do it alone. Our grace-giving, sovereign God will take your lunch and feed the multitudes. He'll take your cookie and open the doors to needy nations. As nanotechnology continues to unfold, let it remind you of the power in small things—including *you*. The face of leadership in the future that has now arrived looks like you!

15

Virtual Reality: Here's Something a Whole Lot Better

THE FUTURE. It's here. Now what?

One of the most fascinating pieces of technology the "future" has brought us is "virtual reality." It may also be one of the most potentially destructive technologies in this cyber age.

Virtual reality is a computer-generated program that claims to deliver experience with new force and format. The experience may be a tour through Windsor Castle or standing at Gettysburg to hear Abraham Lincoln's address or exploring an Amazon jungle. To access the experience, you wear a special headset with a mounted display screen. You hear the sounds and see three-dimensional graphics that deliver the simulation of being in your chosen place.

This experience is not limited. Sensors in the helmet track your eye and head movement. As you turn your head, the sensors feed this information to a computer, which responds by changing the visual and auditory sensation, bringing you the full range of visual and aural stimuli. As technology progresses, the stimuli will increase the sense of being there, and we will be able to choose more places and experiences.

But what long-range effects can this technology have? Where may it possibly lead?

In *Technopoly,* Neil Postman points out that in its developmental stages, technology does not invite a close examination of its consequences. We know technology has improved life. But we do not know where newly developed technology may lead. Postman suggests that technology often begins as a "friend" that asks for trust because of its valuable gifts. Afterward, it may remain a friend, or it may turn into a frightening enemy.

"It is a mistake," Postman writes, "to suppose that any technological innovation has a one-sided effect. Every technology is both a burden and a blessing; not either-or, but this-and-that."[1]

While Postman is not writing about virtual reality specifically, few technological developments more accurately illustrate his thesis. Though it carries potential to enhance our knowledge of history or geography, virtual reality also holds cataclysmic possibility for misuse and damage to human life.

One highly questionable use of virtual reality deals with virtual sex. The technology is being developed to offer an electronically simulated sexual experience. Its developers acknowledge kinky possible uses, but insist it may also offer positive uses in cases of physical impairment or separations of husbands and wives.

Time will tell, but as Postman points out about technology, "the benefits and deficits of such a new technology are by no means distributed equally."

A further precarious aspect of virtual reality lies in the realm of inducing people to settle for simulation in life, in place of what is genuine. To what extent might we find contentment in imitations and fabrications? Might we arrive at the place where we are so comfortable with the counterfeit that we no longer insist on reality or responsibility in other dimensions of life?

Already the movie and television industries have taken us far down this road. When a young woman was raped and killed outside a New York apartment building, several people observed the event from their apartment windows, but no one called the police. Sometime later, 20 people watched without helping as a deaf woman was fatally stabbed on a city thoroughfare.

Psychologists said it was a "bystander intervention

problem," a fear of what getting involved might require of them. But were they afraid, or were the observers so accustomed to a drama world that they were comfortable being only spectators to real tragedy? Had they lived so long in simulated worlds that they could treat reality as little more than theatrics? How much farther down this road might virtual reality carry us?

In God's plan and provision, reality is infinitely sacred and better than even the best simulated experience. "I have come that [you] may have *life,* and *have it to the full"* (John 10:10, emphasis added). Every day people discover this as their lives connect with Him.

One fascinating characteristic of a relative postmodern world is the quest for sensory realities and experiential validations. Peter Senge suggests this fact is the reason Buddhism attracts many young adults. They imagine that Buddhism's history, teachings, and trappings elevate experience. Yearning for something beyond cold doctrine, they look to other realms for satisfaction. They think with their emotions, yearn for special relationships, and churn in quest of the right experience. This fact is influential as churches grapple over kinds of music and worship to model. We can hope that churches will exercise care to maintain the soul and core principles of worship and mission as they process these concerns.

It is timely in the arrival of such a future to follow its "now what?" concerns into deep reflections on the word and promise of the magnificent Jesus. There we learn that our grace-giving, sovereign God offers more than simulated or virtual (contrived) reality. His history enables individuals to become authentic persons of the highest order. His is more than sensory or psychological manipulation. His is reality that translates spunky reality into ennobling hope, into growing stability, and into gutsy joy in a gritty world.

In recent years I have listened to generation Xers and young baby boomers acknowledge their admiration for "real" people. "Why can't people who claim to follow Jesus be more authentic?" they ask. Wherever I have found congregations sprinkled with "real people," I have found healthy congregations who were growing and effectively incorporating these young adults into their fellowship.

What does it mean to possess the reality that is so much better than virtual reality, the reality that flows with spiritual maturity and authenticity?

1. It means facing who and what we really are—turning from sin and self-centeredness and reaching the One who makes His followers more than they would ever be otherwise.

2. It means genuinely taking "self" off the throne of life and giving Jesus permanent residence.

3. It means commencing the unfolding discovery that comes as a person loves God with every capacity of mind and heart and body.

4. It means letting His love flow through our lives to those around us, giving care, respect, kindness to neighbors—remembering our neighbors are any people our lives can touch.

5. It means learning to love myself in a wholesome way.

6. It means ending a life practice that plays favorites, seeking instead to treat each person with respect and dignity.

7. It means caring enough to cry with hurting people and to become Jesus to people in every way I can.

8. It means cultivating a lifestyle that practices courtesy. It means giving the person to whom I'm listening deserved attention. It means unpatronizingly hugging people when they are unhuggable.

9. It means always laboring to expand my circle of friendships.

10. It means taking time to stoop to speak to a child.

11. It means being natural in how I communicate with those around me.

12. It means thinking more about Jesus and praying that I may look more like Him to my world.

13. It means not being defensive, but learning to laugh at myself and seeking to better understand myself.

14. It means regularly decompartmentalizing and decluttering my life to maintain and practice a disciplined life.

15. It means checking over how I've done at the close of every day and asking God's forgiveness wherever I've failed.

16. It means knowing I'll never "bat a thousand" on this, but still reaching beyond where I am, and, however I've failed before, to return to bat!

There is such a difference between computer-generated or human-imagined virtual reality and the reality Christ imparts. He does so much more than any production of self or technology. Our grace-giving, sovereign God provides the best possible "now what" for this world of future which has arrived.

"What is REAL?" asked the Velveteen Rabbit one day. . . . "Does it mean having things that buzz inside you and a stick-out handle?"

"Real isn't how you are made," said the Skin Horse. "It's a thing that happens to you. When a child loves you for a long, long time, not just to play with, but really loves you, then you become real."

"Does it hurt?" asked the Rabbit. "Sometimes," said the Skin Horse, for he was always truthful. "But when you are real you don't mind being hurt."

"Does it happen all at once, like being wound up," he asked, "or bit by bit?" "It doesn't happen all at once," said the Skin Horse. "You become. It takes a long time. That's why it doesn't often happen to people who break easily, or have sharp edges, or who have to be carefully kept. Generally, by the time you are real most of your hair has been loved off, and your eyes drop out and you get loose in the joints and very shabby. But these things don't matter at all, because once you are real, you can't be ugly except to people who don't understand."[2]

PART 4

■

God and I
Are Unbeatable
Partners

*No pessimist ever discovered the secrets
of the stars, or sailed to an uncharted land,
or opened a new heaven to the human spirit.*
—Helen Keller

*The future lies before you,
like paths of pure white snow.
Be careful how you tread it,
for every step will show.*
—Source Unknown

I'm a hostage here for hope, not doom.
—Acts 28:20, TM

■

Dialogue in Real Time

Well, A.D. 2001-plus, I feel better! Many things are uncertain, but many good things have been and are being done already. Nor is some elitist group required to do it. Mustard seeds work. And I am a mustard seed.

Best of all, I see I am not alone in this endeavor. My grace-giving, sovereign God is with me. And I get to be His partner. I have resigned as a pessimist, or as my family's resident doubter. I will bring my doubts to God and let Him hold them for me. Whatever handicaps I face are not sufficient to put Him, and me with Him, out of business.

I'm seeing that my limited resources are not the determining factor for the future. God only asks for "my lunch" as Jesus did of the little boy. Jesus did the rest. Jesus fed all the hungry people. That boy came out well! He gave his lunch away and had more to eat than he would have had if he had kept it for himself.

God makes an unbeatable partner. So, don't get cocky, A.D. 2001-plus. God is in charge and you will never put Him out of business. In fact, why not get on board?

16

In Any Millennium or Century: The Best Place on Earth to Live

THE MISSIONARY COUPLE sitting before the institutional board had just returned from a term in one of the world's politically explosive places.

Civil war had broken out around their mission school and station. For days, two warring factions, one on each side of them, had exchanged bullets and explosives, with them caught in the middle. Night and day, they heard the whistle of weaponry over their home. Both warring factions acknowledged the value of the mission station and school and avoided shooting them.

The missionary family was advised to leave the station, but they were trapped. I was amazed as I listened to them tell of this traumatic experience. They calmly reported how they adjusted to the inescapable. They spoke of their peace, of God's presence, and of the children's ability to play amid the explosive sounds and sights.

One board member pressed, "But how could you stand being in that situation? How did you keep from sheer panic?"

I will never forget their calm answer. "We knew we were there because we'd followed God's will in our lives and for our family. That and our previous experiences had clearly taught us *the safest place in the world is the center of God's will."*

Where will we be able to find the safest home and the most stable place of sanity in the future? *The best and safest place in the world is the center of God's will.* Whatever the explosive nature of life around us, His will is safety and sanity.

Three hundred years ago Benjamin Schmolck pastored a small parish in Germany. One day, a fire burned the parish to the ground. In the following months, his wife and daughter died. Then paralysis struck him, and even his eyesight began to slowly disappear. In the world of his unspeakable tragedy, he penned lines that became one of the church's early hymns, "My Jesus, as Thou Wilt." Benjamin Schmolck wrote:

My Jesus, as Thou wilt. Oh, may Thy will be mine!
Into Thy hand of love I would my all resign.
Thro' sorrow or thro' joy, conduct me as Thine own,
And help me still to say, "My Lord, Thy will be done."
My Jesus, as Thou wilt. Tho' seen thro' many a tear,
Let not my star of hope grow dim or disappear.
Since Thou on earth hast wept and sorrowed oft alone,
If I must weep with Thee, "My Lord, Thy will be done."
My Jesus, as Thou wilt. All shall be well for me;
Each changing future scene I gladly trust with Thee.
Straight to my home above, I travel calmly on,
And sing in life or death, "My Lord, Thy will be done."

Benjamin Schmolck believed the safest place in the world is the center of God's will.

How chaotic is your world? How chaotic is the world around us? We need a strong partner who is resourceful, faithful, and enduring. We need a partner who has proven to have interest in us and integrity. We have a Partner like that, our grace-giving, sovereign God. With such a Partner, I can survive any circumstance of life.

May this always be my residence in the 21st century! May this be my motto and conviction! It is true without exception: *The safest place in the world is the center of God's will.*

17

There Is a Future and a Hope

FOR MANY YEARS I have belonged to the World Future Society, a stimulating global consortium of educators, social scientists, corporate leaders, United Nations personnel, and those from other professions.

At one annual meeting, the luncheon featured an address by a United Nations official. Most of the tables held 10 people, but as I arrived I saw one table set for only two people with a gentleman already occupying one chair. He warmly invited me to join him.

We exchanged names and I learned he was a professor of criminology in a nearby state university. He then added, "I am also a secular humanist and an atheist." He then asked, "And what do you do?"

I smiled and said, "Well, you have quite a partner to share this lunchtime with today. I direct a 21st-century research institute, developing data on how my church denomination can most effectively engage the 21st-century culture, and I am a believer in Jesus Christ, attempting to be a practicing Christian."

I told him I was an ordained minister and had served as my denomination's global missions director. "We have church presence—compassion ministries, educational ministries, Bible-teaching ministries—in more than 100 countries."

He received my lengthy response with friendly interest. Then he added lightly, "I want you to know, you people scare the hell out of me."

In the spirit of our deliberate repartee, I said, "Well, you know, that's one of the things we have in mind."

We both chuckled, and I added, "But, tell me, why do we scare the hell out of you?"

He said, "If we secular humanists and atheists don't get with it, you people will take over the whole world."

I said, "Well, you know, we have that in mind too." Again, we both chuckled.

I was really beginning to like this man. I have learned across many years that open, relaxed, nondefensive, humor-inclusive interchange is a disarming and valuable asset for effective communication!

Our conversation continued and as we approached the end of our meal, I spoke more seriously, asking if I might ask him a special question. "I do not have many opportunities to converse like this with such educated [he had three earned Ph.D. degrees] and gracious secular humanists and atheists as you, and there is a question I've always wished I might ask such a person. It is this: Is there anything in your philosophy of life that leaves you less satisfied than you wish it did?"

He received my question graciously and quickly gave a succinct, open response. "Yes," he said, "there is something. As an atheist, there is no hope."

The immediacy and vulnerability of his statement almost took my breath away. The expression in those deep-set eyes showed me that he had pondered this. His honest statement affirmed what I had begun to believe—that here was a man who though dramatically different in philosophy of life from me possessed a deep sense of honor and honesty.

The gavel sounded and a voice instructed the assembly to prepare to give their attention to the speaker. I realized I had only moments left in this privileged visit. Impulsively, I reached across the table and laid my hand on top of his. I said, "May I tell you this one more thing? I know your philosophy of life is different from mine, and I respect that every individual has the privilege to formulate his own belief system. Whatever you may think of my philosophy of life, however, I would like you to know that it has given me so much hope that sometimes I scarcely know what to do with all of it. I live in an atmosphere that is a constant, satisfying, and healing hope. I only wish we had more time to talk about that."

The speaker began his address, but before my friend turned to listen, he laid his other hand on top of mine, and said, "Yes, I also wish we had more time to talk about this."

As the meeting ended 45 minutes later, my tablemate quickly left. To my dying day I will remember the longing and suffering his voice had earlier confessed. I will remember how with all the extensive and rational parameters of his brilliance and knowledge, he was still missing something fundamental, and he knew it. I will remember his acknowledgment that he might know more about this missing life quality that is, indeed, humanity's greatest quest—the quest for hope.

No human lives without a sense of hope. If we try to live without hope, we live with a deep, unfulfilled ache in the center of our lives.

Those of us who have discovered Jesus Christ have discovered the source and the secret of hope. We have this new century's greatest and strongest asset within our possession.

In a dark time of his life, the apostle Paul was a prisoner. Indeed, from that imprisonment, he never again walked the earth as a completely free man. It was the beginning of the end, and deep inside he knew it. But as that imprisonment separated him from his beloved work, friends, and freedom, he confessed his deep conviction. In reality, it was not unique to him or to that moment and circumstance. It is as timeless as tomorrow. It is alive in this future that is now, a future that asks so penetratingly "now what?" It is the truth that has been affirmed repeatedly through God's Word and across the long journeys of history for men and women everywhere. To whatever extent the culture of any day attempts to build imprisoning walls around a person of faith, that person can respond with all confidence and certainty as Paul did: *"I am a prisoner here for hope, not doom."*

Paul had this further enlightening word for Timothy, his son in the gospel: "I know whom I have believed, and am convinced that he is able to guard what I have entrusted to him for that day" (2 Tim. 1:12).

A new and strikingly different day has dawned in human life. Some people are meeting its change and challenge with a cynical though usually nervous "So what?"

Authentic believers in Jesus Christ, through His hope, can pose a better response. They have found life that can be undeterred by transition. Expecting to be God's positive agents in this new culture, they turn determined faces to the future, and looking to Him they ask, "Now what?" Belief in their grace-giving, sovereign God energizes their actions. In the unbeatable partnership with Him, they confront their world with authentic hope and love. And sure enough, their world with all its blemishes becomes a better place.

So will it be until Jesus returns to do away with evil and to set up His everlasting kingdom.

As you began this adventure, I asked you to read aloud and contemplate a special affirmation. Now I ask you to embrace this affirmation again.

God and I together can and will make it.
We will form an unbeatable partnership
through all that confronts me now, and
through whatever lies beyond the horizon tomorrow!

The future. It's here. So what? Now what?
Grace-giving, sovereign God is your best friend. Walk with Him into your tomorrow world with confidence!

Notes

Preface
1. Randall P. White, *The Future of Leadership* (Washington, D.C.: Pitman Publishing, 1996), xi.

Chapter 1
1. Peter Large, *The Micro Revolution Revisited,* quoted in Richard Saul Wurman, *Information Anxiety* (New York: Bantam Books, 1990), 35.

2. Quoted in *CyberDictionary: Your Guide to the Wired World* (Boston: Wordworks, 1996), 49.

Chapter 2
1. William Strauss and Neil Howe, *Generations: The History of America's Future* (New York: William Morrow Publisher, 1991); Strauss and Howe, *The Fourth Turning* (New York: Broadway Books, 1997).

2. Quoted in an interview article in the *Kansas City Star,* 23 October 1999, 22.

3. *Kansas City Star* article, 26 September 1999, K-1.

Chapter 3
1. Alvin and Heidi Toffler, *Creating a New Civilization: The Politics of the Third Wave* (Atlanta: Turner Publishing, 1995), 36.

2. Richard Slaughter, *The Foresight Principle* (Westport, Conn.: Praeger Press, 1995), 44.

Chapter 5
1. Henry Blackaby, "Who Holds the Future?" *Current Thoughts and Trends* 16, No. 1 (January 2000): 2.

2. Ibid.

Chapter 6
1. Leonard Sweet, *SoulTsunami* (Grand Rapids: Zondervan, 1999), 112.

2. David Limerick and Bert Cunningham, *Managing the New Organization* (San Francisco: Jossey-Bass Publisher, 1993), 43.

Chapter 7
1. Gerald Celente, *Trends 2000* (New York: Warner Books, 1997), 14.

2. Faith Popcorn, *Clicking* (New York: HarperCollins Publisher, 1996), 125-45.

Chapter 8
1. Charles Handy, *The Age of Paradox* (Boston: Harvard Business Press, 1994), x.

2. From address by Circuit Judge Roy Moore at Hillsdale College, printed in monthly college publication *Imprimas* 28, No. 8 (August 1999), 2.

Chapter 10

1. Walter Lord, *The Good Years* (New York: Harper Brothers Publishers, 1960).

2. Arnold Mitchell, "Nine American Lifestyles—Values and Societal Change," printed in Edward Cornish, ed., *The 1990s and Beyond* (Bethesda, Md.: World Future Society Press, 1990).

Chapter 11

1. Tom Sine, "Shifting into the Future Tense," *Christianity Today,* 17 November 1989, 21.

2. George Hunter's book *How to Reach Secular People* (Nashville: Abingdon Press, 1992) is of classic value in the subject of understanding and reaching "secular people."

3. *Current Thoughts and Trends,* July 1997, 25.

4. Slaughter, *Foresight Principle,* 44.

Chapter 12

1. Mark Sullivan and Dan Rather, *Our Times* (New York: Scribner, 1996), 36 ff.

2. Ibid., 132.

3. Dennis F. Kinlaw, *The Mind of Christ* (Nappanee, Ind.: Francis Asbury Press, 1998); Christian A. Schwarz, *Natural Church Development: A Guide to Essential Qualities of Healthy Churches* (Carol Stream, Ill.: ChurchSmart Resources, 1996).

4. Leonard Sweet, *Explorer, e-notes for the Emerging Church,* No. 12, June 5, 2000.

5. Bill Hybels, *Rediscovering Church* (Grand Rapids: Zondervan, 1995), 16.

Chapter 13

1. From address by Richard Foster delivered at Point Loma Nazarene University, San Diego, January 1995.

Chapter 14

1. Warren Bennis, "The Secrets of Great Groups," *Leader to Leader Journal,* Winter 1997.

2. James O'Toole, *Leading Change* (San Francisco: Jossey-Bass Publisher, 1996), 1-36.

Chapter 15

1. Neil Postman, *Technopoly* (New York: Vintage Books, 1993). The cited quote is part of Postman's theses at the beginning of the book (p. 5), but the concept constitutes a theme carried throughout the book.

2. Margery Williams Bianco, *The Velveteen Rabbit* (New York: Alfred A. Knopf, Inc., 1983), 12-14.